Lyric and Dramatic Poetry
1946–82

By Aim

*Translated by Clayton Eshleman
and Annette Smith*

Introduction by A. James Arnold

CARAF BOOKS

The University Press of Virginia

CHARLOTTESVILLE

This is a title in the CARAF BOOKS series

THE UNIVERSITY PRESS OF VIRGINIA
This translation and edition
Copyright © 1990 by the Rector and Visitors
of the University of Virginia

First Published 1990

Et les chiens se taisaient Copyright © Présence Africaine, Paris, 1962.
moi, laminaire . . . Copyright © Editions du Seuil, 1982.
The essay entitled "Poésie et connaissance" is taken from AIME CESAIRE:
L'HOMME ET L'OEUVRE (Présence Africaine, Paris, 1973).
The translation "Poetry and Knowledge" that appears in this volume
first appeared in *Sulfur,* Copyright © *Sulfur* 1982.

Library of Congress Cataloging-in-Publication Data

Césaire, Aimé.
[Selections, English & French, 1990]
Lyric and dramatic poetry, 1946–82 / by Aimé Césaire ; translated
by Clayton Eshleman and Annette Smith ; introduction by A. James
Arnold.
p.   cm. — (CARAF books)
English and French.
Contents: Poetry and knowledge — And the dogs were silent — Moi,
laminaire.
ISBN 0-8139-1256-3. — ISBN 0-8139-1244-X (pbk.)
1. Césaire, Aimé—Translations, English.   I. Eshleman, Clayton.
II. Smith, Annette (Annette J.)   III. Title.   IV. Series.
PQ3949.C44A24   1990
841—dc20   CIP

Printed in the United States of America

Contents

Contents

Contents

viii

Contents

Contents

quand Miguel Angel Asturias disparut
when Miguel Angel Asturias disappeared

Wifredo Lam
Wifredo Lam

Contents

Introduction

Aimé Césaire and Léopold Sédar Senghor emerged as the fore-most francophone black poets during the two decades fol-lowing the end of the Second World War. Unlike his friend Senghor—the cofounder of the negritude movement, whose selected poems and essays have been available in British edi-tions for some time—Césaire has until recently been known worldwide for one long poem, the *Cahier d'un retour au pays natal* (Notebook of a return to the native land).[1] The narrative thrust of the *Cahier* and the presumption that its references to historical personages and events ought to be read discur-sively have contributed to an image of Césaire as primarily a socially committed poet whose material was anticolonialist. This reading of the *Cahier*, which is both aesthetically limiting and historically dominant, resulted in the conviction that, once independence had been largely achieved in Africa and the Caribbean during the 1960s, Césaire was no longer rele-vant. A period of disinterest set in, from which Césaire's work has only lately begun to emerge. Readers of poetry in English did not have access to first-rate translations of Césaire's poetry

1. The original French edition of the *Cahier* was published bilingually in New York by Brentano's in 1947 under the title *Cahier d'un retour au pays natal: Memorandum on My Martinique*. It included an English translation by Lionel Abel and Ivan Goll and a preface by André Breton. The preface was retained in the first Paris edition, published by Bordas a few months later in 1947, which introduced modifications in the text of the poem. The text of the *Cahier* published in the Paris magazine *Volontés* in August 1939 constitutes a preoriginal version. In 1971 Présence Africaine published a new bilingual edition with a revised English translation by Emile Snyder.

until early in the 1980s, when Clayton Eshleman and Annette Smith published *The Complete Poetry* at the University of California Press.[2] Shortly thereafter a selection of Césaire's poetry, translated with extensive scholarly annotations by Gregson Davis, testified both to the importance of Césaire as a poet and to renewed interest in his work in North America.[3] This delay in translating Césaire's poetic oeuvre has meant that his range and significance as a poet could not be adequately judged by readers of English until some fifteen years after the first translations of his theater appeared.[4] Furthermore, two very significant parts of Césaire's early and late poetry have remained unavailable in English until now. They are the dramatic poem *Et les chiens se taisaient,* here translated as *And the Dogs Were Silent,* and *moi, laminaire . . . (i, laminaria . . .).* The composition of the dramatic poem dates from the war years, during which Césaire practiced a surrealist poetic conceived as a "miraculous weapon." Indeed, *Et les chiens se taisaient* is contemporaneous, in its original version, with the collection *Les armes miraculeuses* (The miraculous

2. Aimé Césaire, *The Collected Poetry* (Berkeley, Los Angeles, and London: University of California Press, 1983). This bilingual edition of all the poetry except *Et les chiens se taisaient* and *moi, laminaire . . .* has a reliable bibliography of editions and good comments on Césaire's titles (pp. 20–24). It follows the text of the *Oeuvres complètes* edition of the *Poésies* (Paris; Fort-de-France: Désormeaux, 1976). The original edition of *moi, laminaire . . .* (Paris: Seuil, 1982) was published six years after the so-called *Oeuvres complètes.*

3. Aimé Césaire, *Non-Vicious Circle: Twenty Poems of Aimé Césaire,* translation, introduction, and commentary by Gregson Davis (Stanford, Calif.: Stanford University Press, 1984). Davis's selection is representative of all the collections except *Les armes miraculeuses* and *moi, laminaire . . . ,* which appeared after his translation was completed.

4. Aimé Césaire, *A Season in the Congo,* trans. Ralph Manheim (New York: Grove Press, 1970). Césaire's play *A Tempest: Based on Shakespeare's "The Tempest"—Adaptation for a Black Theater* was published in Richard Miller's translation by Ubu Repertory Theater Publications, New York, in 1986. A curiosity of the Grove Press editions in English is that the text of neither *A Season in the Congo* nor *The Tragedy of King Christophe* (1969) corresponds to any French edition, since Ralph Manheim translated from then-current playscripts.

Introduction

weapons) (1946), of which it constituted the concluding sec-
tion.[5] *Les armes miraculeuses* envisions a cultural revolution
that Césaire at the time believed must both precede and condi-
tion any eventual political liberation of African Americans
throughout the hemisphere and of black people throughout
the world. Moreover, as a collection of poetry, *Les armes mi-
raculeuses* remains incomplete without *And the Dogs Were
Silent*. Read in the context of the original 1946 edition, the
dramatic poem recapitulates and clarifies the overall mythic
structure of the whole.[6]

Césaire published *moi, laminaire . . .* in 1982, more than
twenty years after *Ferrements* (*Ferraments*). That the Paris
edition of *moi, laminaire . . .* received little fanfare and still
less serious critical attention is symptomatic of France's in-
ability to come to terms with the implications of the continu-
ing dependent status of Martinique, Guadeloupe, and French
Guiana. This state of affairs is especially unfortunate because
moi, laminaire . . . contains some of Césaire's most moving
and mature poetry. It also constitutes a poetic retrospective of
a major artist's career. This edition presents *i, laminaria . . .*
bilingually so that the reader who has some French may work
from Eshleman and Smith's English to the original and back
again. Such a reading will, in fact, provide the greatest aes-
thetic satisfaction while reminding the reader that the book is
itself part of a process of cross-cultural exchange.

The text of *Et les chiens se taisaient* that Clayton Eshleman
and Annette Smith have translated is the 1976 version of the
so-called theatrical arrangement of the poem. It is a slightly

5. *Et les chiens se taisaient* was an integral part of *Les armes miraculeuses*
both in the original edition (Paris: Gallimard, 1946) and in the same pub-
lisher's "definitive" edition of 1970, although the text for the theater had
been published separately in 1956 by Présence Africaine. Both texts were
subtitled *tragédie*.

6. My treatment of *And the Dogs Were Silent* both as tragic myth and as
a recapitulation of the structures of *Les armes miraculeuses* can be con-
sulted in *Modernism and Negritude: The Poetry and Poetics of Aimé Cé-
saire* (Cambridge, Mass., and London: Harvard University Press, 1981),
pp. 113–24. The present essay develops other aspects of the question.

modified version of the 1956 and 1962 editions, which marked Césaire's first attempt to write for the stage while remaining firmly anchored in a poetic diction and a lyrical mode of expression.[7] Thus, the CARAF Books edition of *And the Dogs Were Silent* incorporates Césaire's last revisions of a text that remains very close, in most respects, to its origins. Césaire has referred to it as his lyrical oratorio, which is as good a way as any to designate the nature of its structure, texture, and poetic qualities.[8]

Césaire's upbringing

Aimé Césaire belongs to a generation of poets, playwrights, and orators born in various parts of the French empire who were educated in France under a colonial policy of providing an elite to administer the overseas colonies. He was born in Martinique, French West Indies, in 1913, the second child of an employee in the local administration of taxation, which is to say that the Césaires enjoyed a semblance of middle-class respectability in relation to the vast majority of black agricultural workers in the island economy. All of his siblings received a solid education, and several completed university degrees. One sister became a magistrate in colonial Dakar, Senegal, and a brother taught pharmacology at the University of Dakar. Césaire was himself destined to occupy a similarly honorable post in the colonial educational establishment. He was selected as a scholarship student for the Lycée Louis-le-Grand in Paris, where he prepared for the Ecole Normale Supérieure—the institution that has molded the elite of French higher education since Napoleon's day—from 1932 to 1935. Césaire spent the middle years of that decade absorbing the

7. The 1976 Désormeaux edition of *Les armes miraculeuses* in *Poésies,* volume one of the *Oeuvres complètes,* was the first to drop *Et les chiens se taisaient* from the collection. This explains the absence of *And the Dogs Were Silent* from the Eshleman and Smith edition of *The Complete Poetry.*

8. Césaire used the term "oratorio lyrique" to designate *Et les chiens se taisaient* in interviews with Thomas A. Hale in July 1972. See Hale's 1974 University of Rochester Ph.D. dissertation "Aimé Césaire: His Literary and Political Writings, with a Bio-Bibliography" (Ann Arbor, Mich.: University Microfilms, 1976), p. 125.

masterworks of French and European literature and thought, which he was expected to later dispense to other young colonials like himself.

What could not have been foreseen by the colonial administration that recruited Antillean students like Césaire was that those students would become conscious of themselves as blacks having something in common with Africans, whom they had been encouraged to look down upon by virtue of their own very tenuous but much longer connection to French culture. When one considers the negritude movement with the full benefit of hindsight more than a quarter-century after the decolonization of most of the African continent, the process that began when Césaire, Léon-Gontran Damas, and Léopold Sédar Senghor met as students in Paris may seem to bear the mark of historical necessity. It would, however, be both facile and erroneous to assume that the affirmation of African values that resulted directly from their association as young writers and intellectuals represented a continuous and uninterrupted process from colonization and subjection to decolonization and freedom. The problematic relationship of a heroic persona, lyric or dramatic, to the mass of colonized people is at the heart of the question. The negritude movement as we find it expressed in Césaire's lyric and dramatic poetry of the 1940s had a distinctly heroic cast to it, but the experience was one of self-knowledge experienced as intense suffering rather than one of joy. The suffering was to be transmuted by Césaire in the form of a heroic persona, the Rebel in *And the Dogs Were Silent*, who attains the status of culture hero only at the sacrifice of his own life. He is a salvatory mythic figure for whose characteristics Césaire borrowed amply from Egyptian, Greek, Christian, and doubtless other traditions as well. Overall, the poem has an apocalyptic tone and atmosphere. Allusions to judgment abound. The Rebel has visions of spiritual and natural reconciliation in an indeterminate future. Within a historical perspective on the negritude movement, examined in relation to the ongoing process of decolonization that is, of course, far from complete, *And the Dogs Were Silent* epito-

Introduction

mizes a crucial moment in the coming to consciousness of Cé-
saire's generation of black intellectuals *as colonized black in-
tellectuals*. This dramatic poem has proved to be prophetic in
a way not intended by the author. Rather than serving as a
signpost or a map to a radiant future, *And the Dogs Were Si-
lent* functions now as the sign of the sacrifice of Césaire's gen-
eration to the very process of decolonization that they were
the first to envisage collectively and globally.[9] There is bitter
irony in the fact that the process of decolonization was never
really begun in the French West Indies, where Césaire has
been an elected official since 1946 as mayor of Fort-de-France,
Martinique. The reader who comes to *i, laminaria* . . . di-
rectly from *And the Dogs Were Silent* will better understand
the restrained elegiac mood of Césaire's last collection of
poetry, which can be said to express the realization that Mar-
tinique (along with Guadeloupe and French Guiana) passed
directly from colonial to neocolonial status. In this fundamen-
tal respect the sacrifice of the Rebel in *And the Dogs Were Si-
lent* was politically in vain. Finally, these two works conceived
nearly forty years apart constitute a poetic testament in which
politics is never the subject, but instead remains a permanent
ghostly presence.

Our culture is coextensive with our language. For Césaire
the literary language was French. His cultural options, even
those he saw as revolutionary in the 1940s, were limited by
his relationship, as a colonized Martinican, to the structures,
the range, and the traditions of French language and litera-
ture. During Césaire's formative years Creole, the mother
tongue of Martinicans, was not available to him as a writer.[10]

9. See Arnold, *Modernism and Negritude*, pp. 269–72.
10. Césaire was manifestly irritated by the questions put to him by
Jacqueline Leiner concerning his apparent refusal to express himself in
Creole at the time of *Et les chiens se taisaient*. Concerning the fact that the
magazine *Tropiques* was written in French, he said of himself and the other
contributors: "we wouldn't have been capable of writing it in Creole. That's
all there is to it! I don't even know if it's conceivable." (my translation). See
"Entretien avec Aimé Césaire par Jacqueline Leiner" in the reedition of
Tropiques, vol. 1 (Paris: Jean-Michel Place, 1978), p. x.

Introduction

Suffice it to say here that Creole was so thoroughly stigmatized by its origins in slavery that no serious writer of Césaire's generation could consider using it other than to retell folktales in verse or to write verse in the manner of folktale.[11] Edouard Glissant has traced the modern cultural history of Martinican Creole as a vehicular language in *Caribbean Discourse,* which is today the best book on the subject.[12] If we are always in language, then the language we are in goes a long way toward defining our cultural identity. Indeed, our cultural conflicts will be expressed in our relationship to language if, like Martinicans, we exist in a conflictual state between two or more languages. For Césaire, being already in the language of the French university system when he became conscious of himself as a colonized black was a major feature of the dilemma. Negritude as an articulate effort to break out of the fetters of the colonizer's language into Africanness was ultimately doomed to failure. The Africanness that the negritude movement posited as an ideal was an abstraction from the beginning. Negritude was useful, even necessary, as long as it was possible to articulate the cultural project as a global opposition to the colonialist enemy. But when the battle for decolonization had been won, when new nation-states had been created in Africa and the Caribbean, the fundamental opposition that grounded negritude in present reality disappeared. That is precisely when Césaire stopped publishing lyric poetry. It is notable that *i, laminaria . . .* is written in a new idiom forged out of the realization that the cultural project of negritude had been superceded.

His essay "Poésie et connaissance" (Poetry and knowledge), which appeared in the January 1945 issue of *Tropiques*—the

---

11. An example of La Fontaine's fables retold in Martinican Creole can be found in Marie-Thérèse Julien Lung-Fou's *Fables créoles* (Fort-de-France, Martinique: Editions Dialogue, 1958). In *Fab' Compè Zicaque* (Paris: Horizons Caraïbes, 1958) Gilbert Gratiant—who had been Césaire's English teacher—undertook to write socialist poetry on the model of Creole tales.

12. Edouard Glissant, *Caribbean Discourse,* CARAF Books (Charlottesville: University Press of Virginia, 1989), pp. 123–34, 182–94.

magazine edited in Fort-de-France between 1941 and 1945 by
Césaire, his wife Suzanne, René Ménil, and colleagues at the
local lycée—contextualizes the French West Indian negritude
movement better than any other single document. It is pre-
sented in English in toto following this Introduction. "Poetry
and Knowledge" combines a rapid overview of modernism in
France with a credo and an ars poetica. It was written at the
same time as *And the Dogs Were Silent* and is the best intro-
duction to its poetics. The essay—originally a paper read at a
meeting of philosophers in Port au Prince, Haiti, on 28 Sep-
tember 1944—is constructed on a series of oppositions that
were designed to suggest a new reordering of human en-
deavor. "Poetry and Knowledge" declares its fundamental
ideological agreement with the program of André Breton's
surrealist movement. Descartes is to be subverted by Freud.
French rationalism is to be short-circuited by the miraculous
weapons of the unconscious. Furthermore, a collective uncon-
scious that Césaire has never disavowed is presumed to pro-
vide access to an archaic and universal knowledge. Rudiments
of C. G. Jung's theory of the collective unconscious were ap-
parently available to Césaire at second hand, to judge from
the rough version of it he presented in "Poetry and Knowl-
edge." This would explain his taking Jung to be a German
philosopher rather than the Swiss practitioner of depth psy-
chology that he was. Césaire's understanding of Freud and
Jung only makes sense, however, in the context of his reliance
on Nietzsche's affirmation of life. In Césaire's claim that since
1850 French culture had abandoned its Apollonian reliance
on form in favor of Dionysian vitalism, one finds the Mar-
tinican writer sidestepping the Freudian death instinct that
would be fundamental to a later French reading of Freud
promulgated by Jacques Lacan.[13] "Poetry and Knowledge" is
positively mainstream as a reading of the modern tradition

13. *Modernism and Negritude* (pp. 85–88) contextualizes a reading of
Césaire's poem "Les Pur-Sang" (The thoroughbreds), in terms of the sur-
realists' reading of Freud. Ronnie L. Scharfman has given a post-Lacanian
reading of similar phenomena in her *"Engagement" and the Language of*

in French poetry, beginning with Baudelaire and extending through Rimbaud and Lautréamont to Apollinaire and Breton. The rhetorical thrust of "Poetry and Knowledge" is pedagogical and hortatory rather than analytical. The amalgam of anti-rationalist positions that it articulates can be summed up in the proposition that myth is superior to science: "Only myth satisfies mankind completely; heart, reason, taste for detail and wholeness, taste for the false and the true, since myth is all that at once, a misty and emotional apprehension, rather than a means of poetic expression . . ."

If a preference for myth—or what Harry Levin called pseudo-myth—over history is one of the characteristics of modernist culture, then *And the Dogs Were Silent* deserves to be examined as an important modernist work.[14] It needs to be read both with an eye to the mythic plot structure Césaire incorporated in it and, finally, in a postmodern spirit of ideological critique. Confusion still reigns over the significance of negritude as a cultural movement, especially in the anglophone world, and a better understanding of *And the Dogs Were Silent* will help to dispel it. Césaire's dramatic poem is the most complex and the most complete representation of negritude as a cultural project that he ever undertook. The limitations and weaknesses inherent in his vision of heroic negritude are here made apparent in ways that permit us to read all his early poetry in a new critical perspective.

And the Dogs Were Silent contains the element of a syncretic myth, the purpose of which is to link the Caribbean present to an African past. Creatures from the island environment of Martinique are related to their analogues in antiquity: the hawk and the dog are the most notable. Dogs were the

the Subject in the Poetry of Aimé Césaire, University of Florida Monographs, Humanities number 59 (Gainesville: University of Florida Press, 1987), pp. 24–28.

14. Harry Levin, "Some Meanings of Myth," in *Myth and Mythmaking,* ed. Henry A. Murray (Boston: Beacon Press, 1968), pp. 111–12. *Modernism and Negritude* (pp. 50–54) lays out the principal reference points on myth and history in the context of literary modernism.

allies of the masters in hunting down runaway slaves, the ma-
roons; thus, dogs—particularly barking dogs—represent im-
minent and ignominious death: "Look, they've torn him to
pieces . . . they the dogs / they the men with bloody lips, with
steel eyes but you know what I am telling you: judicial func-
tion is finished." This speech from act one, spoken by the Sec-
ond Tempter's voice, relates the dogs to men with bloody lips,
both in the past of slavery and in the present time of colonial
exploitation. It also evokes the judicial function of dogs, an
oblique and encoded reference to the dog- or jackal-headed
god Anubis who, in the Egyptian *Book of the Dead,* both
leads the deceased to the last judgment and performs the "ju-
dicial function," weighing the heart of the deceased on a scale.
Césaire slyly told Rodney E. Harris that the dogs in the title of
the oratorio may have been derived from Egyptian mythology,
but, he implied, since he was relying on surrealist automatic
writing at the time, who can tell?[15] The evidence within the
play is such that little doubt remains.

In the same scene the Rebel speaks of the assassination
of the sun, whereas the Second Tempter's voice replies that
"they've torn him to pieces . . . like a wild pig, like an agouti!
like a mongoose!" Once again the animals denote humble re-
ality in the Caribbean; but the "him" that presumably desig-
nates the imminent fate of the Rebel becomes homologous
with Osiris in the same mythological context. Osiris, the civi-
lizer of the Egyptian world, was torn to pieces by conspirators
led by his brother Set after his return from a mission to Asia.
Césaire's Rebel ascribes a similar civilizing function to him-
self. "I had brought this land to the knowledge of itself, ac-
quainted this land with its own secret demons. . . ." Some-
what earlier, the Chorus had answered the First Madwoman's
question ("Where is the one who will sing for us?") in this
manner: "He holds a snake in his right hand, in his left a mint
leaf, his eyes are sparrow hawks his head a dog's head." The
snake represents the Uraeus of Egyptian mythology, the sa-

15. Rodney E. Harris, *L'humanisme dans le théâtre d'Aimé Césaire*
(Sherbrooke, Quebec: Naaman, 1973), p. 28.

cred asp that destroys the sun-god's enemies. The sparrow hawk evokes Horus, the posthumous son of Osiris; and the dog's head brings one back to Anubis, who was revered for inventing embalming when he reunited the dismembered parts of Osiris that had been scattered over the Nile Valley. At the very beginning of act one the architect's "crab scuttle words" can be read allegorically as the action of the Nile crab, *oxyrhyncus*, which is said to have eaten the phallus of Osiris and to have been abhorred for that sacrilege. The architect functions analogously as the colonialist enemy in Césaire's parody of contemporary reality.

Shortly after its evocation of the Uraeus, Horus, and Anubis, the Chorus identifies "the one who will show us the road" as an African fertility god: "With your sandals of rain and courage, ascend, appear, imminent / lord . . . , come up in the desert like water . . . / ascend, most imminent lord, flesh whirls in the shavings of dark Africa." Even the date of the Rebel's death in November corresponds to the tradition handed down by Plutarch, according to whom Osiris was killed on the seventeenth day of the month Athyr, which corresponds to mid-November in the Julian calendar.[16] J. Viaud has summed up the attributes of Osiris very much as Césaire has depicted the Rebel in *And the Dogs Were Silent:* "As a vegetation spirit that dies and is ceaselessly reborn, Osiris represents the corn, the vine and trees. He is also the Nile which rises and falls each year; the light of the sun which vanishes in the shadows every evening to reappear more brilliantly at dawn."[17] For Césaire, Senghor, and their friends in the Paris of the 1930s

16. See *Plutarch's Morals*, ed. W. W. Goodwin, vol. 4 (1870; Boston: Little, Brown, 1874), p. 76. Véronique McNelly first suggested to me the importance of the *Book of the Dead* for the symbolism of *Et les chiens se taisaient* in a graduate seminar in 1987. I have also drawn on references she has found in Sir J. G. Frazer, *The Golden Bough*, 1 vol. abridged ed. (New York: Macmillan, 1951), pp. 422 (date of the death of Osiris); 451 (symbolism of anemones and violets); 449 (identification of Dionysus with Osiris).

17. J. Viaud, "Egyptian Mythology," *New Larousse Encyclopedia of Mythology* (London and New York: Prometheus Press, 1970), p. 17.

Introduction

Egypt was Africa, and Egyptian civilization as we know it was understood by them to have been the heir of ancient Nubia. Ultimately, Cheik Anta Diop would systematize this principle of the negritude movement in his book *Nations nègres et culture.*[18] A Ghanaian scholar, Albert Owusu-Sarpong, has devoted several good pages of his book on Césaire's theater to the view of ancient Egypt as an African civilization.[19] This tradition in scholarship begins with the Greeks—Herodotus, Lucian, Aeschylus in *The Suppliant Maidens,* Diodorus, and Strabo—and was taken up again at the beginning of this century by Leo Frobenius, whose galvanizing effect on the poets of negritude is now well known. In *And the Dogs Were Silent* Césaire sought to stimulate the cultural and spiritual renewal of the African diaspora using the materials at hand. In the vocabulary of Claude Lévi-Strauss this is a poetics of *bricolage,* a do-it-yourself cultural project.

Césaire's demonstrable reliance upon details of the story of Osiris is evidence of an effort to construct his lyric oratorio on a syncretic myth. On occasion he uses details borrowed from the myths relating the fate of other vegetation spirits. In the Rebel's line (act one) "Violets anemones are springing up with each step of my blood . . ." we encounter the flowers engendered by the blood of Adonis and Attis, respectively. These divergent details are not meant to confuse but rather to complete symbolically the impression of the sacred unity between the Rebel and nature, as opposed to the unnatural principle of colonial order that oppresses and kills him. The careful reader will be able to adduce many other connections with these and possibly other mythic figures who must die for the renewal of their community.

Readers of *The Birth of Tragedy* will understand that Césaire was working out a tragic plot in accordance with Nietz-

18. Cheik Anta Diop, *Nations nègres et culture* (Paris: Présence Africaine, 1954).
19. Albert Owusu-Sarpong, *Le temps historique dans l'oeuvre théâtrale d'Aimé Césaire* (Sherbrooke, Quebec: Naaman, 1986), pp. 81–84.

sche's interpretation of the sacrifice of Dionysus.[20] Nietzsche's
book on tragedy had a massive impact on literary modernism,
particularly in articulating a tragic sense of life that frequently
expressed itself in literary forms other than drama. We now
know that Césaire used *The Birth of Tragedy* as a means of
relating certain myths taken from antiquity to the tragic ac-
tion of *And the Dogs Were Silent*. His statement to Rodney E.
Harris was unusually candid in this regard.[21] In the same in-
terview Césaire declared that it was the barbarity, as he saw it,
of early Greece that interested him, because of its proximity to
Africa. Césaire may well have read French scholars who had
pointed out that the myth of Dionysus appeared to be a
double of the Osiris myth. At all events he was prepared to
make the association of Dionysus (via Nietzsche) to Osiris
and other gods of annual renewal whose trace occurs in *And
the Dogs Were Silent*. The references to the Osiris myth are so
numerous as to indicate that Césaire wanted them recognized
as a counterbalance to the suggestion of a specifically Chris-
tian sacrifice. Thus, the use of the adjective *Christophoric* by
the Rebel in act one, in the context of a West Indian planta-
tion economy based on slave labor, both recalls the name of
Christ and displaces it by allusion to the Haitian hero King
Christophe, not to mention the Roman prince of the eighth
century who is identified in Eshleman and Smith's note. A
single word serves to situate the dramatic poem's relationship
to Christianity in colonial society. The fact that Césaire spe-
cifically associates the adjective *Christophoric* with the slaves
as a group, a community of the oppressed, is scarcely ade-
quate, however, to establish a link between the Rebel and the
anonymous mass of agricultural laborers whose suffering he
represents in exemplary fashion. One may also see this stylistic

20. *Modernism and Negritude* develops in some detail this last aspect of
Césaire's dramaturgy in *And the Dogs Were Silent,* but with explicit refer-
ence to Nietzsche's favorite example, *Oedipus Rex.* (pp. 114–18).

21. Rodney E. Harris cites a January 1969 interview with Césaire to this
effect in *L'humanisme dans le théâtre d'Aimé Césaire,* p. 28.

Introduction

device as the sign of the separation between the tragic hero and the group rather than as the sign of their unity.

Césaire systematically parodies Christian institutions throughout *And the Dogs Were Silent.* The bishops in full regalia are clearly presented as mad representatives of colonialism, differing from other colonialists—the Great Promoter or the Administrator, for instance—only in their degree of irresponsibility. As early as 1950, in his *Discours sur le colonialisme* (Discourse on colonialism), Césaire had treated Christian religious institutions in the colonies as the historical auxiliary of slavery, racism, and cultural extermination. His corrosive treatment of Catholic saints and the Virgin Mary in *Les armes miraculeuses* convinced many readers that Césaire must be an antireligious writer. The evidence to the contrary is very strong. Césaire in *Et les chiens se taisaient* was trying, desperately it would seem, to salvage a sense of authentic religious feeling and of belonging to the natural world that Christianity no longer offered to West Indian intellectuals like himself. He consequently turned the modern movement in poetry toward a spiritual goal. His strategy in *Et les chiens se taisaient* was to construct a symbolic tragic action on a syncretic master plot of sacrifice and renewal.

All the Europeans in Césaire's lyrical oratorio are one-dimensional and have more than a little in common with the parodic imperialists created by Alfred Jarry in his 1896 play *Ubu roi* (King Ubu). They are so conceived that the audience or reader cannot possibly take them seriously as rounded characters. The Administrator in *And the Dogs Were Silent* mouths the platitudes that were to be found in much self-serving government rhetoric about the necessity of saving the savages from themselves. God gave the colonies to Europeans so as to restore them to "universal movement": "Moreover it is debatable whether there is in the world apart from ourselves any people who think, I mean really think, who do not ruminate the confused mingling of a few vapid ideas brought back to the lower brain still warm from their breathing or their sleep." This speech sums up nicely the thesis of the primitive mind propounded by Lévy-Bruhl (and whose late recantation colonialists were quick to forget). Césaire doesn't miss the opportunity to do a variation on Kipling's "white man's burden" at the end of the same speech. The Administrator and the bishops are presented—and disposed of—soon after the curtain rises, so as to set the stage for the sacrificial drama of negritude. All the references to Osiris that were discussed above are introduced gradually, following the parody of colonial institutions. The break in tone that this dichotomous worldview entails is, of course, extreme, and it works against successful staging of the dramatic poem as theater. If the parodic scenes work on the stage, then the lyrical solos, duets, and the pieces written for several voices seem stilted. If the lyrical tone is established as the norm for a kind of sumptuous, coloratura poetry, then the parodic scenes are likely to appear flat or out of place. It is the high style of Césaire's language that brings to mind the vocabulary of grand opera. But in his representation of the colonialists Césaire has provided scenes from opera bouffe. On stage these two styles work against one another. Césaire was obviously aware of this problem when he told Harris that *Et les chiens se taisaient* should be played in mask, a recommendation that Jarry had also made for his *Ubu roi*. The mind of a reader, however, is perfectly able to keep these two styles separate or, rather, to play them against one another for harmonic contrast. The lyrical intensity of the speeches of Rebel, Lover, Chorus, and Choristers allows for little aesthetic distancing by the reader. We experience them close up. Their rhythms wash over us like melodic waves. We swim mentally in the winedark sea of Césaire's extremely rich language. The style is hot. The colonialists are depicted in a cool style, on the other hand. They are distanced from us in the extreme. The scene in which the Great Promoter warms up the engine of empire recalls one of Jarry's most famous inventions in *Ubu roi*, the debraining machine. But Césaire's character is taken as the parodic representative of a real political system that was still very much alive when his lyrical oratorio was written. "Track down, track down / throughout the lands, the seas, the air, wind up, wind up, / squeeze, squeeze . . . There . . . steady! / Let no clod of earth remain untrampled, undug, uncultivated. / Squeeze, squeeze . . ." The rapacious greed of imperialism is immediately present in this passage. In "Poetry and Knowledge," which follows very closely the argument of Breton's second manifesto of surrealism, this corrosive, expressionist style is attributed to Lautréamont: it "dissolves with its blowtorch" of humor the cruel obscenity of colonialism. Césaire's originality was to invite the reader to experience these two worldviews as irreconcilable, rather than to suggest a reasoned response to colonialism. This unresolved dialectic of colonialist and colonized, with its clear implication that the Rebel holds the key to all that is fundamentally and eternally human, is a perfect representation of Césaire's negritude as an ideological position. In *Et les chiens se taisaient* he envisaged the identity of the African American in such a way that the only access to African roots necessarily runs through tragic myth. The result is aesthetically satisfying, if one can accept Césaire's premise; but it is socially problematical in that it offers no access to political solutions to African American problems. Objections to *Et les chiens se taisaient* have regularly drawn their ammunition from the political argument. It would be fairer to Césaire and to *Et les chiens se taisaient* to ask why he was unable, in the 1940s and 1950s, to write more politically for the theater.

Edouard Glissant has written extensively on myth, history, and literature in the French West Indies in an effort both to establish the grounds for a new Caribbean historiography and to situate myth—especially tragic myth—in this context. He observes that "in myth (as in tragedy which for the Greeks originated in myth) the achievement of collective harmony assumes the ritual sacrifice of a hero, at the very least his apparent failure. This sacrifice is the veil behind which revelation is fulfilled: it is a distracting image that conceals the meaning of the mythic or tragic act, while consecrating it." Glissant cites René Girard's *Violence and the Sacred* as a major statement of the theory of the "'sacrificial victim' as the basis for history."[22] Such myths, and the tragedies modeled on them, mediated between the law of nature and the exigencies of culture.

In Césaire's vision of tragic myth there is a gulf between the order of nature—to which the Rebel and his ritual sacrifice belong, hallowing his relationship to the black world—and the order of contemporary culture, however perverse, that Césaire represents as belonging to the masters of colonial empire. More accurately, as the preceding analysis of Césaire's syncretic master plot has shown and a careful reading of "Poetry and Knowledge" will confirm, his tragedy is designed to convey the feeling that the black world, through the ritual sacrifice of the Rebel, has access to a more ancient, and presumably truer, cultural order that has been disrupted by Europe since the Renaissance and its voyages of exploration, discovery, and conquest. Insofar as Prometheus has become the archetypal culture hero of Western civilization, Césaire's Rebel represents an anti-Prometheus who is tortured and condemned to death by the representatives of a modern technological culture. *And the Dogs Were Silent* tells us not only that colonialism and its attendant racism were wrong but that the philosophical and scientific postulates pressed into their service must be combatted as well. This is the ultimate justification for Césaire's peremptory dismissal of scientific method and Aristotelian logic in "Poetry and Knowledge." Césaire knew full well what the powers of reason are, in their systematic formulations from Aristotle to Kant—who is the butt of his jibes on the transcendent and the immanent—because his own mind was their product, albeit an illegitimate colonial product.

Césaire's bitterness toward Europe and its institutions is so acerbic because his was the first generation of French West Indian intellectuals to realize that they were not French, and that they were not French because they were black. Césaire treated this realization discursively in his introduction to the 1960 Paris edition of Bertène Juminer's novel *Les bâtards*

22. Glissant, *Caribbean Discourse*, p. 72.

Introduction

(The bastards).[23] Juminer's novel is a bildungsroman that traces the coming to consciousness of the next generation of French West Indians, who read Césaire alongside Jean-Paul Sartre. Sartre's novel *Nausea* figures prominently in *Les bâtards;* it establishes the climate of existentialist thought that conditioned the early work of Fanon and Glissant, as well as Juminer and others. French West Indians, in the view of both Césaire and Juminer, are the bastard offspring of the European father who will not recognize them and the African mother from whom they have turned away. *Et les chiens se taisaient* in 1946 reconstructed Mother Africa as the matrix of a tragic myth, part of whose purpose is to deny henceforth the unloving father, Europe.

It is the presumed underlying unity of the black world in *And the Dogs Were Silent* that accounts for the depiction of certain dramatic details—the murder of the master that brings about the downfall of the Rebel, for instance—as West Indian, whereas other details are represented as distinctly African. At the beginning of act three a similar device unites the names of African and North American rivers—the Congo and Mississippi—around the image of slave labor: "The race made of dirt the race in the dirt discovered it had feet / let the Congo and Mississippi flow with gold / flow with blood / the race made of dirt, the race made of ashes is walking / the feet on the road explode into saltpeter bits." Later in act three "a cortege from medieval Africa pours out onto the stage: a magnificent reconstitution of ancient Benin civilization." Why Benin? surely because of the Benin bronzes, of which more than two thousand were shipped to Britain in the wake of the British punitive expedition of 1897. The furor and confusion caused by the revelation of this high art form thriving in black Africa long before the colonial period was a serious challenge to official imperialist racism, which required that subject

23. Cited by Keith Q. Warner in his introduction to his translation of Bertène Juminer, *The Bastards*, CARAF Books (Charlottesville: University Press of Virginia, 1989), p. xxx.

Introduction

peoples be represented as primitives so as to justify their sub-
jugation. These and other suggestions of an African atmo-
sphere are dramaturgical rather than historical. They serve to
extend to the entire black world a master plot the elements of
which can be seen as African only if one accepts the ancient
tradition that Egypt was African and, by extension, that the
Dionysian mystery religion of Eleusis was a Greek adaptation
of the Osiris cult. Only a poet of Césaire's accomplishment
could have taken such a gamble and won. His extraordinary
success in *And the Dogs Were Silent* testifies to the strength of
his will as a poet and to the sustained qualities of voice he has
distributed over a number of supporting roles. The variously
designated characters who function as parts of a polyphonic
chorus are best considered in terms of the vocal texture of the
whole work. It is no exaggeration to say that in his lyrical or-
atorio Césaire attempted to restore to the logos its sacred
function. How one is to judge the meaning of this feat in the
broader cultural context is another question, however.

Again it is Glissant in *Caribbean Discourse* who provides
the most productive theoretical position. "If it is ridiculous to
claim that a people 'has no history,' one can argue that, in cer-
tain contemporary situations, while one of the results of
global expansion is the presence (and the weight) of an in-
creasingly global historical consciousness, a people can have
to confront the problem posed by this consciousness which it
feels is 'vital,' but which it is unable to 'bring to light': because
the lived circumstances of this daily reality do not form part of
a continuum, which means that its relation with its surround-
ings (what we would call its nature) is in a discontinuous rela-
tion to its accumulation of experiences (what we would call its
culture)" (p. 61). It would be hard to present the problematics
of *And the Dogs Were Silent* more succinctly. Glissant adds
that "in such a context, history as far as it is a discipline and
claims to clarify the reality lived by this people, will suffer
from a serious epistemological deficiency: it will not know
how to make the link." *And the Dogs Were Silent* is posited
upon this epistemological deficiency; the inability to link na-

ture and culture discursively from the perspective of the colonized French West Indian involves a creative leap into tragic myth as a substitute for an impossible historiography.

The final upward-surging movement of the oratorio gives the last word to the Narrator and Narratress, who lyrically fuse their identity with the islands: "Orgy, orgy, divine water, star of luxurious flesh, vertigo / islands cool rings on the ears of plunging sirens / islands coins fallen from the star-filled pouch." And finally: "I come to you" with its antiphonal response: "Islands, I am one of you!" This orgiastic fusion of identities invites the reader to imagine a quasi-mystic oneness that implicitly excludes the historical imagination. As for the Rebel, we can see him before the lofty portal where he will be judged by an African Anubis before joining the immortals: "Bark dogs guardians of the lofty portal." In *Modernism and Negritude* (pp. 118–19), I describe this paroxystic conclusion as the transformation of the consciousness of the two narrators, who abandon the critically conservative discourse of the Chorus to express the creative energy and vision of the Rebel, which had been communicated to them by his ritual sacrifice.

This visionary representation of the French West Indian's experience relied heavily on the antihistorical, mythologizing strain within modernism that Renato Poggioli identified as agonistic.[24] *Et les chiens se taisaient* expressed a fully developed version of modernist agonism, which was coextensive with negritude as a cultural project in the 1940s.

Reading *i, laminaria . . .* after *And the Dogs Were Silent* allows one to measure the limitations of the negritude movement while at the same time appreciating the maturation of a major poet. The contrast between the two works is great on all levels: the claims made for the lyrical voice; the scope and representation of time and space; the personal and poetic bestiary; the sense of the sacred and its efficacity.

---

24. Renato Poggioli, "Agonism and Futurism," *The Theory of the Avant-Garde,* Icon editions (New York: Harper & Row, 1971), pp. 60–77.

moi, laminaire

Introduction

A greater modesty prevails in *i, laminaria* . . . , a more convincing and appealing sense of self as well. As he approached age seventy, Césaire was able to articulate movingly his feeling of loss and his sense of failure or of misdirected energies. Something of the elegiac voice was already present in *Ferrements;* but a new poetic diction emerged as the collection *moi, laminaire* . . . took shape. The poems are less dense than were those in *Les armes miraculeuses* because the model of metaphoric composition has changed. At the same time the poems in *moi, laminaire* . . . are both more terse and more accessible. The mystery of surrealist associative metaphor—in retrospect one may be tempted to say its function as mystification—has given way to an allusiveness that no longer claims to be in direct communication with the most ancient lore of the species. The pressure of historical forces since 1946 has resulted in a more concise poetic language, a paring down and a peeling away of the rhetorical flourishes that made *Et les chiens se taisaient* such a richly textured work of art: "the atmospheric or rather historic pressure / even if it makes certain words of mine sumptuous / immeasurably increases my plight" ("Lagoonal Calendar").

Césaire in *moi, laminaire* . . . knows that he can communicate more by saying less. The initially strange title, with its studied use of lowercase typography—more common in American than in French poetic practice in this century—signifies in the most material way a reduction of the sense of self. But this humbler self is very tenacious in holding onto its bit of volcanic rock in the Caribbean Sea. In the poem "algae" the laminarian alga, a rudimentary marine plant, declares its vulnerable nakedness ("the main thing is to sniff nakedly / to think nakedly"). Resurgence is represented as a function of the tradewinds, the tides, and the strength of the earth. No heroic persona is present. The Rebel—and his equally heroic successors Christophe and Lumumba—have been written out of the scene. The laminarian alga is here so thoroughly a part of the natural whole that it does not and cannot affirm itself as a grammatical subject. In terms of the nature/culture debate

Introduction

in "Poetry and Knowledge," nature is still supreme and the poet's allegiance to its force is stronger than ever. In this respect there is remarkable continuity between the lyrical oratorio and the late lyric. The identification with the plant, more particularly with the tree, in "Poetry and Knowledge" lent grandeur to the lyrical self. The laminarian alga reduces that self to the relative dimension of a speck, while maintaining the essential structure of its identity.

The first poem in *i, laminaria . . . ,* "Lagoonal Calendar," and the liminary prose that precedes it are concerned with a new ordering of space and time. We learn at the outset in 1982 that it is: "Time also to settle one's account with a few phantoms and a few ghosts." The laminarian self declares: "i inhabit from time to time one of my wounds / each minute i change apartments." The cosmic time of tragic myth has given way to a succession of discrete moments, and the space belonging to the self has become a series of precarious havens. The transcendent spiritual goal of the Rebel is now "an abandoned cult," and the "Vision of the blue Caribbean spangled with gold and silver islands in the scintillation of the dawn"— the didascalic note that closes *And the Dogs Were Silent*—is, in the "Lagoonal Calendar," an "avatar / of an absurdly botched version of paradise."

West Indian literature in French has evolved a geographic symbolism in which the principal towns, and the coast on which they are located, represent the repressive order of colonialism, which comes from the sea. The hills—the mornes— are a refuge. There the runaway slaves—the maroons—sought individual freedom or set up autonomous communities from the earliest times of settlement in the West Indies. In Jamaica and the Guyanas a remote hinterland permitted the establishment of maroon republics. The smaller islands colonized by France (Haiti was already independent after 1804) did not have a vast, uncolonized hinterland. Their geography has been reduced in the literary imagination to the coast, with its dangers, and the mornes as a promise of precarious individual

Introduction

freedom. Both Edouard Glissant in *La Lézarde* (The ripening) and *Le discours antillais* (Caribbean discourse)[25] and Daniel Maximin in *L'isolé soleil* (Lone sun)[26] develop this symbolism to explain important aspects of French West Indian history. The literary imagination has served to transmit an anguished sense of the precariousness of freedom as lived experience and as an ideal in the French West Indies. The special conditions of their history, which did not result in the military expulsion of colonialism, as in Haiti, or a successful long-term resistance to colonialism, as in Jamaica or the Guyanas, have contributed to the dialectic of nature and culture that we see in Césaire's poetry from *Et les chiens se taisaient* to *moi, laminaire.* . . . For the Martinican poet, culture, as the privilege and the weapon of the colonialist, belongs to the coast and to the towns. It is marked with the sign of mortal danger. Culture (in which term we read, historically, European culture) must be subverted. This is the origin of Césaire's notion of marooning (*marronner*) the West. In *Et les chiens se taisaient*, at the inception of the heroic phase of the negritude movement, that subversion was unable to transcend the nature/culture dialectic in the direction of history. Therefore it sought transcendence in an Africanized syncretic myth that imitated the rituals at the root of all the former slave religions of plantation society—voudou, *santería*, macumba—in which these oppressed communities found collective survival mechanisms. In the French West Indies, however, these cults did not survive into the twentieth century, as they did in Haiti, Cuba, and Brazil. Nor did the French West Indies see the invention of a new, syncretic religion like Rastafarianism in Ja-

25. J. Michael Dash has some good pages on the symbolism of landscape in the introduction to his translation of Edouard Glissant, *The Ripening* (London and Kingston: Heinemann Caribbean Writers Series, 1985), pp. 1–3. Glissant elaborates this symbolism more fully in *Caribbean Discourse*, pp. 10–11.

26. Daniel Maximin, *Lone Sun*, CARAF Books (Charlottesville: University Press of Virginia, 1989), pp. 36–39.

maica. Consequently, salvatory myth in Martinique could only take the form of individual poetic utterance, as it did in Césaire's lyrical oratorio.

There is ample evidence in *i, laminaria* . . . that its author knows all this. Moreover, the meaning of the collection as a work expressing a moment in the poet's consciousness should, I think, be understood as a deconstruction of the negritude myth. Deconstruction functions here as ideological demystification, a laying bare of the structures of identity within negritude as a cultural project, while denying its claim to a transcendent truth. Thus *i, laminaria* . . . deconstructs "Poetry and Knowledge" as well.

Césaire in *i, laminaria* . . . has found a new space to signify his own cramped, stultifying position in a neocolonial Martinique—the mangrove swamp. One might expect the brackish waters of the mangrove swamp, at the point of contact between land and sea, inside and outside, us and them, to represent the positive dialectical transformation of opposites that would result in a personal and poetic, if not a collective, liberation. This was the role Césaire assigned to the virgin forest (practically nonexistent in Martinique, of course) in *Les armes miraculeuses.* In "Another Season," the poem that follows "The Virgin Forest" in *The Collected Poetry,* Césaire attributed resurgence and renewal to "the volcanoes" and "the horsemen of sperm and thunder" (p. 131). Not so in *i, laminaria.* . . . In the poem entitled "mangrove swamp," Césaire has used the marginality of this typical Caribbean geographical feature as the site or locus of a self-examination in which he is not gentle with his own heroic persona as we have seen it in *And the Dogs Were Silent.* The mornes have lost their dynamic potential to represent the energy of rebellion: "it is not always a good idea to wallow in the torpor of mornes." The polysemic syncretic myth of the lyrical oratorio is reduced to "gnoseological contemplation" in which "it is not always good to lose oneself." The same criticism is directed against the fascination with "genealogical trees (the risk being to realize that one went astray at the worst possible crossroad of evolution)." If the poet of "mangrove swamp" is no longer "the dying warrior no one sees fall," he once was, or rather the Rebel was the hero playing the agonistic game of Maré Maré. Césaire has entitled "the mangrove swamp syndrome" the new condition in which the pitch-black surface mirrors the nature of French West Indian survival. It is a postmodern *mise en abyme*,[27] a surface without any real depth that permits one to observe the structures of one's condition: "Mephitic. Mud-bottomed." It mirrors an illusion: "The look is that of forests. / The lulling / that of the swaying of tides." The adjective "limp" (*mou*) occurs twice, at the beginning and at the end of this short poem. The "limp flag of all the surrenderings" echoes intertextually the rallying cry in "Poetry and Knowledge": "It's not fear of madness that will oblige us to furl the flag of imagination." No, it is no longer fear of madness but the dead weight of history that brings the poet of "the mangrove swamp syndrome" to conclude: "It is quite possible to survive limp / by anchoring oneself in the commensal mud." But what sort of anchor is provided by a mirror? The Protean eel of the mangrove swamp can only recall Proteus, god of transformation, in a derisive mode; if "the fruit floats" and "the fish climbs the trees," neither of these apparently surrealist metaphors any longer contains the energy of a revolutionary transformation of existence. As Ihab Hassan put it in a recent reassessment of the "postmodern perspective": "Postmodernism vacates the traditional self, simulating self-effacement—a fake flatness, without inside/outside—or its opposite, self-multiplication, self-reflection." An important point to bear in mind, however, when applying First World literary theory to a Third World context (it is impossible to take seriously here the fiction that Martinique is an integral part of France) is that creators of art in the Third World cannot entirely forget that the dispersion of the self they express can never quite be reduced to "the play of language," al-

27. See Lucien Dällenbach, *Le récit spéculaire: essai sur la mise en abyme* (Paris: Seuil, 1977), pp. 9–11.

though their represented self may diffuse "itself in depthless styles, refusing, eluding, interpretation."[28] The stakes are immeasurably higher in the Third World, where it is reasonable to fear the obliteration of entire cultures. Edouard Glissant in *Caribbean Discourse* argues eloquently that the French West Indies may be facing a slow cultural death by asphyxiation.[29]

In an interview that Césaire gave to Daniel Maximin on the occasion of the publication of *moi, laminaire* . . . he addressed this question with specific reference to "Lagoonal Calendar": "at a time when I feel the French West Indian 'self' is threatened, surrounded, nibbled away, at a moment when I have the impression that the clock is running out, I experience a sense of tragedy and it's at these moments that one holds tight to oneself and the recourse to poetry under the pressure of history seems to me to be the essential recourse." The sense of tragedy, then, stood at the inception of *i, laminaria* . . . but it does not occupy the center stage, histrionically, as it does in *And the Dogs Were Silent.* Replying to Maximin's comparison of the modest laminaria with the splendid tree of his early work, Césaire attributed the essential difference to the experience that separates old age from the great lyrical flights of youthful confidence: one begins the poetic life as Icarus but winds up struck down (*foudroyé*) or at least "brought back to harsh reality."[30] The comparison with Icarus, who flew too close to the sun, is telling. The solar myth is another constant in Césaire's poetic oeuvre, and in this case he used it to explain the substitution of the humble laminaria for the noble tree. Thirty-five years of political life as deputy and mayor of Fort-de-France, and all the disappointments and dashed hopes that those years represent, are summed up in the laminarian self.

Césaire developed at some length in the interview with

28. Ihab Hassan, "Pluralism in Postmodern Perspective," *Critical Inquiry* 12 (Spring 1986): 505.

29. Glissant, *Caribbean Discourse,* p. 169.

30. Aimé Césaire, "La poésie, parole essentielle," *Présence africaine* 126 (1983): 9, 11 (my translation).

Introduction

Daniel Maximin what the sacred meant to him. "We are people of the sacred. I am not an initiate; I am an initiate through poetry, if you like, and I believe I am a man of the sacred. The Martinican sacred, the French West Indian sacred exists; it has become trite, of course, it has been occulted, ignored, and sometimes so terribly distorted that we ourselves either misunderstand it or misjudge it, but I believe it is there" (p. 21). He then related an anecdote concerning his discovery, on a visit to the Casamance district of Senegal with André Malraux, that a Martinican carnival mask representing an ox head exists in Senegal as well. His Senegalese guide explained that it was the mask worn by initiates, whereas in Martinique a very similar mask frightened children during carnival. Césaire explained the perversion of the sacred in Martinique in this way: "And here was the drama of history: at home it had become the devil; in other words, it is as though the god of the vanquished had become the devil of the victor" (p. 21). Small wonder that Césaire in his youth had set out in search of the old gods and in the hope of rehabilitating them.

In the poem "ibis-Anubis" we see Césaire returning to the old gods, but his former faith has left him. By uniting the name of Anubis with the ibis, he has recalled the Egyptian tradition according to which the divine ibis created the world and invented the hieroglyph: "the painful signature of a bird / under the incomprehensible alphabets of the moment." Thoth, the ibis-god, was also represented as a baboon with the head of a dog, whence the connection with Anubis in the poem. Thoth was worshipped at Hermopolis Magna as the universal demiurge who created the world by the sound of his voice: "i will never know which words—the first in a message—broke through my throat." The title of the poem raises the veil of mystery that stretched across *Et les chiens se taisaient*. The poet declares—"between allusion and illusion"—how he had constructed his pantheon: "i drew lots for my ancestors for a plenary earth." Now, however, he performs "the rites of shipwreck" toward the end of his "lengthy mangrove swamp maturation." The poem recapitulates an itinerary marked by erosion and corrosion, and ending with a setting sun: "mute the undermining / the assault always deferred / one is permitted to perform the rites of shipwreck." Césaire can only ask, looking back over his explorations of the sacred: "what do i have left today except to ponder / that in the face of destiny in advance i belched a life . . . ?" In "ibis-Anubis" Césaire takes stock of a sacred that had never been other than a supplement, a pseudo-myth, for the poetic communication of what was otherwise lacking in Martinican life.

Not all representations of the sacred in *moi, laminaire* . . . are as negative, however. The ten poems devoted to his friend, the Cuban painter Wifredo Lam, attribute to his work an efficacity that Césaire no longer claims for his own poetry. The Lam poems,—beyond their testimony arising from sincere admiration for an important Caribbean painter—point indirectly to the Martinican's loss of sacred awe, which he nonetheless finds alive in Lam's canvases. In a brief prose text written to introduce Césaire's poetic illustrations of his paintings, Lam relates his work to *santería*, the Afro-Cuban religion, and to Mantonica Wilson, the godmother—mother of the gods—who initiated him into it: "I visited her in her house filled with African idols. She made me the gift of the protection of all these gods. . . ." They are Yoruba gods who have been Creolized in the West Indies: the creator, Olorun; Yemoja, who has become Yemanja, goddess of the sea; Shango, transformed from the nature spirit of thunder and lightning into the god of war; and Ogun's name in Haiti has acquired the redundancy Ferraille (iron) to designate his original attribute as patron of metallurgy. In "tongue fashion" the old obsession with keys to mysteries opens the poem and is followed through with allusions to the *asson* (ritual rattle) of voudou and the diamond-shaped sacred design, or *vèvè*. Lam's style of painting in the 1940s suggested a Creolization of Picasso, whom Lam had known in Paris just before the war. In this context, one may find in Césaire's appreciation of Lam a displacement of conjoined modernism and negritude that, elsewhere in *i, laminaria* . . . , the Martinican poet treats as a shipwreck. The Lam poems close the collection and represent a considerable part of the whole. Careful consideration of Césaire's deconstruction of his former heroic persona in this collection, resulting in the reduced laminarian self, leads to the conclusion that Césaire gives us here the apotheosis of his alter ego, Lam, whose monosyllabic name is also the first syllable of *laminaire*. The poem "tongue fashion" plays on the word *laminaire* in a way that encourages such an interpretation. The words *error* (*erreur*) and *errancy* (*errance*) share a root, and they rime with *aire,* the final syllable of *laminaire*. The laminarian self found the name of this particular alga in order to incorporate into itself the deconstruction of the heroic self's error and its errancy (*errance* echoes the title of the final poem, "Dit d'errance," in Césaire's 1950 collection *Corps perdu* [Lost body]), but also in order to identify itself with the success of Lam: "here begins / reclaimed from wild beasts / the sacred territory reluctantly conceded by the leaves" ("tongue fashion").

The poetic and mythological figure of Thoth, whose trace one finds in "ibis-Anubis," will permit the reader of *i, laminaria . . .* to situate this collection and its author with respect to modernism and the postmodern. Vera Kutzinski found Thoth to be "a figure for the process of supplementation" in Jay Wright's *Dimensions of History* (1976).[31] Her reading of Thoth in *Dimensions of History* follows the lead of Derrida, who sees the Egyptian divinity as presiding "over the organization of death." In his article on "Plato's Pharmacy" Derrida found Thoth to be a protodeconstructionist whose functions are strangely Derridean and eminently postmodern: "Thoth repeats everything in the addition of the supplement: in adding to and doubling as the sun, he is other than the sun and the same as it. . . . He would be the mediating movement of dialectics if he did not also mimic it, indefinitely preventing it, through his ironic doubling, from reaching some final ful-

---

31. Vera Kutzinski, *Against the American Grain: Myth and History in William Carlos Williams, Jay Wright, and Nicolás Guillén* (Baltimore and London: Johns Hopkins University Press, 1987), p. 117.

fillment or eschatological reappropriation. Thoth is never present. Nowhere does he appear in person. No being-there can properly be *his own*." [32]

These details of Derrida's reading of Thoth contrast sharply with the tradition cited above, according to which Thoth was worshipped at Hermopolis Major as the universal demiurge (a creative function that Derrida's text denies to the god). The contrast is an open invitation to examine Césaire's relation to the scribal trace registered by Derrida. In "ibis-anubis" Césaire deplores the failure of the poetics of voice, of the logos, while reiterating its features. Césaire may be postmodern in his deconstruction of negritude, but in his nostalgia for the sacred he belongs to and expresses another world.

Within the group of Lam poems "tongue fashion" calls for a rereading of the collection in terms of the wordplay generated by the term *laminaria*. The reader will find the French text indispensable to this exploration of the dissemination of the poet's soul (*l'âme*) throughout the space (*aire*) of the collection. Even a brief examination will suffice to demonstrate that the term *laminaria* does not conceal a symbol that, properly deciphered, might yield a secret or an original truth. On the contrary, *laminaire* seems to have been chosen by Césaire for its capacity to generate strings of phonetic signifiers and their opposites. If the word *Lam* homophonically suggests soul, it can just as well suggest a sharp blade (*lame*) that cuts into thin strips (*lamine*) the face (*la mine*) of the friend (*l'ami*). The word *laminare* can be read as having blown up (*mina*) the habitat (*aire*) or the eagle's nest (*aire*), in either case the refuge of Cés*aire*. The phoneme *-aire* is contained in the name Cés*aire*; and the word *laminaire* thus unites Lam and Césaire in a fraternal embrace: "the law of your name" ("Wifredo Lam . . ."). The good reader of *moi, laminaire* . . . wanders (*erre*) over this space (*aire*) and errs (*erre*), no doubt, but can a soul do otherwise? This way of rereading *moi, laminaire* . . . syntagmatically points to the impossibility of an ut-

32. Jacques Derrida, *Dissemination* (Chicago: University of Chicago Press, 1981), pp. 92–93.

Introduction

terance that would finally stabilize the self. Poetic mastery is not self-mastery in this retrospective work. The distribution of the disjecta membra of consciousness over the verbal space of the collection is the figurative equivalent of dismemberment (Osiris); but the resurrection (Anubis-Thoth) is no longer an article of faith. Finally, *i, laminaria . . .* is the locus of contradiction in the poet's oeuvre.

ACKNOWLEDGMENTS

A summer stipend from the National Endowment for the Humanities in 1988 facilitated preparation of this introduction. I should like to thank Cynthia Foote and Janet Anderson for the particular care they have taken in the preparation of the manuscript and the production of this book.

A. James Arnold
University of Virginia

*   *   *

The translators would like to thank the National Endowment for the Arts for a translation fellowship in 1988 that enabled them to complete the work on this book.

Poetry and Knowledge

*1944 given in Haiti
as speech*

Poetic knowledge is born in the great silence of scientific knowledge.

Mankind, once bewildered by sheer facts, finally dominated them through reflection, observation, and experiment. Henceforth mankind knows how to make its way through the forest of phenomena. It knows how to utilize the world.

But it is not the lord of the world on that account.

A view of the world, yes; science affords a view of the world, but a summary and superficial view.

Physics classifies and explains, but the essence of things eludes it. The natural sciences classify, but the *quid proprium* of things eludes them.

As for mathematics, what eludes its abstract and logical activity is reality itself.

In short, scientific knowledge enumerates, measures, classifies, and kills.

But it is not sufficient to state that scientific knowledge is summary. It is necessary to add that it is *poor and half-starved.*

To acquire it mankind has sacrificed everything: desires, fears, feelings, psychological complexes.

To acquire the impersonality of scientific knowledge mankind *depersonalized* itself, *deindividualized* itself.

An impoverished knowledge, I submit, for at its inception—whatever other wealth it may have—there stands an impoverished humanity.

In Aldous Huxley's *Do What You Will* there is a very amus-

Poetry and Knowledge

ing page. "We all think we know what a lion is. A lion is a desert-colored animal with a mane and claws and an expression like Garibaldi's. But it is also, in Africa, all the neighboring antelopes and zebras, and therefore, indirectly, all the neighboring grass . . . If there were no antelopes and zebras there would be no lion. When the supply of game runs low, the king of beasts grows thin and mangy; it ceases altogether, and he dies."

It is just the same with knowledge. Scientific knowledge is a lion without antelopes and without zebras. It is gnawed from within. Gnawed by hunger, the hunger of feeling, the hunger of life.

Then dissatisfied mankind sought salvation elsewhere, in the fullness of here and now.

And mankind has gradually become aware that side by side with this half-starved scientific knowledge there is another kind of knowledge. A fulfilling knowledge.

The Ariadne's thread of this discovery: some very simple observations on the faculty that permitted the human whom one must call the primitive scientist to discover the most solid truths without benefit of induction or deduction, as if by flair.

And here we are taken back to the first days of humanity. It is an error to believe that knowledge, to be born, had to await the methodical exercise of thought or the scruples of experimentation. I even believe that mankind has never been closer to certain truths than in the first days of the species. At the time when mankind discovered with emotion the first sun, the first rain, the first breath, the first moon. At the time when mankind discovered in fear and rapture the throbbing newness of the world.

Attraction and terror. Trembling and wonderment. Strangeness and intimacy. Only the sacred phenomenon of love can still give us an idea of what that solemn encounter can have been . . .

It is in this state of fear and love, in this climate of emotion and imagination that mankind made its first, most fundamental, and most decisive discoveries.

Aimé Césaire

It was both desirable and inevitable that humanity should accede to greater precision.

It was both desirable and inevitable that humanity should experience nostalgia for greater feeling.

It is that mild autumnal nostalgia that threw mankind back from the clear light of scientific day to the nocturnal forces of poetry.

Poets have always known. All the legends of antiquity attest to it. But in modern times it is only in the nineteenth century, as the Apollonian era draws to a close, that poets dared to claim that they knew.

1850—The revenge of Dionysus upon Apollo.

1850—The great leap into the poetic void.

An extraordinary phenomenon . . . Until then the French attitude had been one of caution, circumspection, and suspicion. France was dying of prose. Then suddenly there was the great nervous spasm at the prospect of adventure. The prosiest nation, in its most eminent representatives—by the most mountainous routes, the hardest, haughtiest, and most breathtaking, by the only routes I am willing to call sacred and royal—with all weapons and equipment went over to the enemy. I mean to the death's-head army of freedom and imagination.

Prosy France went over to poetry. And everything changed.

Poetry ceased to be a game, even a serious one. Poetry ceased to be an occupation, even an honorable one.

Poetry became an adventure. The most beautiful human adventure. At the end of the road: clairvoyance and knowledge.

And so Baudelaire . . .

It is significant that much of his poetry relates to the idea of a penetration of the universe.

> Happy the man who can with vigorous wings
> Mount to those luminous fields serene!
>
> The man whose thoughts, like larks,
> Fly liberated to the skies at morning,

—Who hovers o'er life and effortlessly harks
To the language of flowers and voiceless things!
—"Elevation"

And in "Obsession":

But the shadows are themselves canvases
Wherein live, welling up in my eye by thousands,
Beings invisible to the familiar gaze . . .

And in "Gypsies on the Road":

Cybele, who loves them, increases her green glades,

Makes rock flow and desert bloom
Before these travelers, for whom
Lies open the familiar empire of future shades.

As for Rimbaud, literature is still registering the aftershocks
of the incredible seismic tremor of his famous *lettre du voyant*
(the seer's letter): "I say that one has to be clairvoyant, to
make oneself clairvoyant."
Memorable words, words of distress and of victory . . .
Henceforth, the field is clear for humanity's most momen-
tous dreams.
There is no longer any possibility of doubt about Mal-
larmé's enterprise. The clear-eyed boldness of his letter to Ver-
laine makes of Mallarmé rather more than the poet whose
shadow is Paul Valéry. Mallarmé is an especially important
engineer of the mind:

Apart from the prose pieces and the poetry of my
youth and the aftermath that echoed them . . . I
have always dreamed of and attempted something
else. . . . A book, very simply, a book that would
be premeditated and architectonic, and not a col-
lection of chance inspirations, even wondrous ones.
I shall go farther; I shall say The Book, persuaded

Aimé Césaire

that at bottom there is only one, that every writer, even the genius, was working at unconsciously. The Orphic explanation of the Earth, which is the poet's only duty. And the literary game par excellence. . . . There you have my vice revealed.

To pass from Mallarmé to Apollinaire is to go from the cold calculator, the strategist of poetry, to the enthusiastic adventurer and ringleader.

Apollinaire—one of the awesome workmen whose advent Rimbaud had predicted—was great because he knew how to remain fundamentally himself in between the popular ballad and the war poem.

You whose mouth is made in the image of God
A mouth that is order itself
Be indulgent when you compare us
To those who were the perfection of order
We who seek adventure everywhere

We are not your enemies
We want to give you vast and strange domains
Where mystery in bloom is offered to whoever would
    pluck it
New fires are found there, colors yet unseen
A thousand imponderable fantasms
That await the conferral of reality
We want to explore goodness an enormous country where
    all is silence
Then there is time that you can banish or call back
Pity for us who fight always on the frontiers
Of the limitless and of the future
Pity our errors pity our sins
                                        —"The Pretty Redhead"

I come now, having skipped a few stops, I confess, to André Breton . . . Surrealism's glory will be in having aligned against it the whole block of admitted and unprofessed enemies of po-

Poetry and Knowledge

etry. In having decanted several centuries of poetic experience.
In having purged the past, oriented the present, prepared the
future.

It was André Breton who wrote: "After all, it is the poets
over the centuries who have made it possible to receive, and
who have enabled us to expect, the impulses that may once
again place humankind at the heart of the universe, abstract-
ing us for a second from our dissolving adventure, reminding
us of an indefinitely perfectible place of resolution and echo
for every pain and joy exterior to ourselves."

And still more significantly: "Everything leads us to believe
that there exists a certain mental point from which life and
death, the real and the imaginary, the past and the future, the
communicable and the incommunicable, high and low, cease
to be perceived contradictorily. And one would search in vain
for a motive in surrealist activity other than the determination
of that point."

Never in the course of centuries has higher ambition been
expressed with greater tranquillity.

This highest ambition is the ambition of poetry itself.

We have only to examine the conditions necessary to satisfy
it, and their precise mode.

The ground of poetic knowledge, an astonishing mobiliza-
tion of all human and cosmic forces.

It is not merely with his whole soul, it is with his entire
being that the poet approaches the poem. What presides over
the poem is not the most lucid intelligence, or the most acute
sensibility, but an entire experience: all the women loved, all
the desires experienced, all the dreams dreamed, all the im-
ages received or grasped, the whole weight of the body, the
whole weight of the mind. All lived experience. All the pos-
sibility. Around the poem about to be made, the precious
vortex: the ego, the id, the world. And the most extraordinary
contacts: all the pasts, all the futures (the anticyclone builds
its plateaux, the amoeba loses its pseudopods, vanished vege-
tations meet). All the flux, all the rays. The body is no longer
deaf or blind. Everything has a right to live. Everything is
summoned. Everything awaits. Everything, I say. The individ-

Aimé Césaire

ual whole churned up by poetic inspiration. And, in a more disturbing way, the cosmic whole as well.

This is the right occasion to recall that the unconscious that all true poetry calls upon is the receptacle of original relationships that bind us to nature.

Within us, all the ages of mankind. Within us, all humankind. Within us, animal, vegetable, mineral. Mankind is not only mankind. It is *universe*.

Everything happens as though, prior to the secondary scattering of life, there was a knotty primal unity whose gleam poets have homed in on.

Mankind, distracted by its activities, delighted by what is useful, has lost the sense of that fraternity. Here is the superiority of the animal. And the tree's superiority still more than the animal's, because the tree is fixed, attachment, and perseverance to essential nature . . .

And because the tree is stability, it is also surrender.

Surrender to the vital movement, to the creative élan. Joyous surrender.

And the flower is the sign of that recognition.

The superiority of the tree over mankind, of the tree that says yes over mankind who says no. Superiority of the tree that is consent over mankind who is evasiveness; superiority of the tree, which is rootedness and deepening, over mankind who is agitation and malfeasance.

And that is why mankind does not blossom at all.

Mankind is no tree. Its arms imitate branches, but they are withered branches, which, for having misunderstood their true function (to embrace life), have fallen down along the trunk, have dried up: mankind does not blossom at all.

But one man is the salvation of humanity, one man puts humanity back in the universal concert, one man unites the human flowering with universal flowering; that man is the poet.

But what has he done for that?

Very little, but that little he alone could do. Like the tree, like the animal, he has surrendered to primal life, he has said yes, he has consented to that immense life that transcends him. He has rooted himself in the earth, he has stretched out

Poetry and Knowledge   ~~free~~

his arms, he has played with the sun, he has become a tree: he has blossomed, he has sung.

In other words, poetry is full bloom.

The blossoming of mankind to the dimensions of the world—giddy dilation. And it can be said that all true poetry, without ever abandoning its humanity, at the moment of greatest mystery ceases to be strictly human so as to begin to be truly cosmic.

There we see resolved—and by the poetic state—two of the most anguishing antinomies that exist: the antinomy of one and other, the antinomy of Self and World.

"Finally, oh happiness, oh reason, I listened to the azure sky, which is blackness, and I lived, a golden spark in nature's light."

So, pregnant with the world, the poet speaks. "In the beginning was the word . . ." Never did a man believe it more powerfully than the poet.

And it is on the word, a chip off the world, secret and chaste slice of the world, that he gambles all our possibilities . . . Our first and last chance.

More and more the word promises to be an algebraic equation that makes the world intelligible. Just as the new Cartesian algebra permitted the construction of theoretical physics, so too an original handling of the word can make possible at any moment a new theoretical and heedless science that poetry could already give an approximate notion of. Then the time will come again when the study of the word will condition the study of nature. But at this juncture we are still in the shadows. . . .

Let's come back to the poet. Pregnant with the world, the poet speaks.

He speaks and his speech returns language to its purity.

By purity I mean not subject to habit or thought, but only to the cosmic thrust. The poet's word, the primal word: rupestral design in the stuff of sound.

The poet's utterance: primal utterance, the universe played with and copied.

And because in every true poem, the poet plays the game of

the world, the true poet hopes to surrender the word to its free associations, certain that in the final analysis that is to surrender it to the will of the universe.

Everything I have just said runs the risk of implying that the poet is defenseless. But that isn't at all correct. If I further specify that in poetic emotion nothing is ever closer to anything than to its opposite, it will be understood that no peacemaker, no plumber of the deep, was ever more rebellious or pugnacious.

Take the old idea of the irritable poet and transfer it to poetry itself. In this sense it is appropriate to speak of poetic violence, of poetic aggressivity, of poetic instability. In this climate of flame and fury that is the climate of poetry, money has no currency, courts pass no judgments, judges do not convict, juries do not acquit. Only the firing squads still know how to ply their trade. The farther one proceeds, the more obvious the signs of the disaster become. Police functions are strangulated. Conventions wear out. The Grammont laws for the protection of mankind, the Locarno agreements for the protection of animals, suddenly and marvelously give up their virtues. A wind of confusion.

. . .

An agitation that shakes the most solid foundations. At the bloodied far end of mortal avenues an immense disloyal sun sneers. It is the sun of humor. And in the dust of the clouds crows write one name over and over: ISIDORE DUCASSE COUNT OF LAUTREAMONT. Lautréamont, the very first in fact, integrated poetry and humor. He was the first to discover the functional role of humor. The first to make us feel that what love has begun, humor has the power to continue.

Sweeping clean the fields of the mind is not the least important role of humor. To dissolve with its blowtorch the fleeting connections that threaten to build up in our gray matter and harden it. It is humor, first and foremost, that makes Lautréamont sure—in opposition to Pascal, La Rochefoucauld, and so many other moralists—that had Cleopatra's nose been shorter, the face of the world would not have been changed;

Poetry and Knowledge

that death and the sun can look one another in the eye; that mankind is a subject empty of errors . . . that nothing is less strange than the contradictoriness one discovers in mankind. It is humor first and foremost that assures me it is as true to say the thief makes the opportunity as: "opportunity makes the thief . . ."

Humor alone assures me that the most prodigious turnabouts are legitimate. Humor alone alerts me to the other side of things.

— We are now arriving in the crackling fields of metaphor.

One cannot think of the richness of the image without the repercussion suggesting the poverty of judgment.

' Judgment is poor from all the reason in the world.
The image is rich with all the absurdity in the world.
Judgment is poor from all the "thought" in the world.
The image is rich with all the life in the universe.
Judgment is poor from all the rationality in existence.
The image is rich with all the irrationality in life.
Judgment is poor from all immanence.
The image is rich with all transcendence.

Let me explain . . .

However much one may strain to reduce analytical judgment to synthetic judgment; or to say that judgment supposes the connecting of two different concepts; or to insist on the idea that there is no judgment without X; that all judgment is a surpassing toward the unknown; that all judgment is transcendence, it is nonetheless true that in all valid judgment the field of trancendence is limited.

The barriers are in place; the law of identity, the law of non-contradiction, the logical principle of the excluded middle.

Precious barriers. But remarkable limitations as well.

It is by means of the image, the revolutionary image, the distant image, the image that overthrows all the laws of thought that mankind finally breaks down the barrier.

In the image *A* is no longer *A*.

Aimé Césaire

You whose many raspberried laughs
Are a flock of tame lambs.

In the image *A* can be not-*A:*

The black focus plate, real strand suns, ah! wells of magic.

In the image every object of thought is not necessarily *A* or
not-*A.*
    The image maintains the possibility of the happy medium.
    Another by Rimbaud:

The carts of silver and copper
The prows of steel and silver
Strike the foam
Raise the bramble roots.

    Without taking into consideration the encouraging com-
plicity of the world as it is either *found* or *invented*, which
permits us to say *motor* for *sun, dynamo* for *mountain,
carburetor* for *Carib,* etc., . . . and to celebrate lyrically the
shiny connecting rod of the moons and the tired piston of the
stars . . .
    Because the image extends inordinately the field of tran-
scendence and the right of transcendence, poetry is always on
the road to truth. And because the image is forever surpassing
that which is perceived because the dialectic of the image tran-
scends antinomies, on the whole modern science is perhaps
only the pedantic verification of some mad images spewed out
by poets . . .
    When the sun of image reaches its zenith, everything be-
comes possible again . . . Accursed complexes dissolve, it's the
instant of emergence . . .
    What emerges is the individual foundation. The intimate
conflicts, the obsessions, the phobias, the fixations. All the
codes of the personal message.
    It isn't a matter, as in the earlier lyric, of *immortalizing* an

hour of pain or joy. Here we are well beyond anecdote, at the very heart of mankind, in the babbling hollow of destiny. My past is there to show and to hide its face from me. My future is there to hold out its hand to me. Rockets flare. It is my childhood in flames. It is my childhood talking and looking for me. And within the person I am now, the person I will be stands on tiptoe.

And what emerges as well is the old ancestral foundation. Hereditary images that only the poetic atmosphere can bring to light again for ultimate decoding. The buried knowledge of the ages. The legendary cities of knowledge.

In this sense all the mythologies that the poet tumbles about, all the symbols he collects and regilds, are true. And poetry alone takes them seriously. Which goes to make poetry a serious business.

The German philosopher Jung discovers the idea of energy and its conservation in Heraclitus's metaphor of the eternally living fire, in medieval legends related to saintly auras, in theories of metempsychosis. And for his part, Pierre Mabille regrets that the biologist should believe it "dishonorable to describe the evolution of blood corpuscles in terms of the story of the phoenix, or the functions of the spleen through the myth of Saturn engendering children only to devour them."

In other words, myth is repugnant to science, whereas poetry is in accord with myth. Which does not mean that science is superior to poetry. To tell the truth, myth is both inferior and superior to *law*. The inferiority of myth is in the degree of precision. The superiority of myth is in richness and sincerity. Only myth satisfies mankind completely; heart, reason, taste for detail and wholeness, taste for the false and the true, since myth is all that at once. A misty and emotional apprehension, rather than a means of poetic expression . . .

Thus, love and humor.

Thus, the word, image, and myth . . .

With the aid of these great powers of synthesis we can at last understand André Breton's words:

"Columbus had to sail with madmen to discover America."

Aimé Césaire

And look at how that madness has been embodied, and lasted . . ."

It's not fear of madness that will oblige us to furl the flag of imagination."

It's not fear of madness that will oblige us to furl the flag of imagination.

And the poet Lucretius divines the indestructibility of matter, the plurality of worlds, the existence of the infinitely small.

And the poet Seneca in *Medea* sends forth ships on the trail of new worlds: "In centuries to come the Ocean will burst the bonds within which it contains us. A land of infinity shall open before us. The pilot shall discover new countries and Thule will no longer be the ultimate land."

"It's not fear of madness that will oblige us to furl the flag of imagination . . ." And the painter Rousseau *invented* the vegetation of the tropics. And the painter de Chirico unknowingly painted Apollinaire's future wound on his forehead. And in the year 1924 the poet André Breton associated the number 1939 with the word *war*.

"It's not fear of madness that will oblige us to furl the flag of imagination." And the poet Rimbaud wrote *Illuminations*.

And the result is known to you: strange cities, extraordinary countrysides, worlds twisted, crushed, torn apart, the cosmos given back to chaos, order given back to disorder, being given over to becoming, everywhere the absurd, everywhere the incoherent, the demential. And at the end of all that! What is there? Failure! No, the flashing vision of his own destiny. And the most authentic vision of the world if, as I stubbornly continue to believe, Rimbaud is the first man to have experienced as feeling, as anguish, the modern idea of energetic forces in matter that cunningly wait to ambush our quietude . . .

No: "It's not fear of madness that will oblige us to furl the flag of imagination . . ."

And now for a few propositions by way of summation and clarification.

Poetry and Knowledge

FIRST PROPOSITION

Poetry is that process which through word, image, myth, love, and humor establishes me at the living heart of myself and of the world.

SECOND PROPOSITION

The poetic process is a naturalizing process operating under the demential impulse of imagination.

THIRD PROPOSITION

Poetic knowledge is characterized by humankind splattering the object with all its mobilized richness.

FOURTH PROPOSITION

If affective energy can be endowed with causal power as Freud indicated, it is paradoxical to refuse it power and penetration. It is conceivable that nothing can resist the unheard-of mobilization of forces that poetry necessitates, or the multiplied élan of those forces.

FIFTH PROPOSITION

Marvelous discoveries occur at the equally marvelous contact of inner and outer totality perceived imaginatively and conjointly by, or more precisely within, the poet.

SIXTH PROPOSITION

Scientific truth has as its sign coherence and efficacity. Poetic truth has as its sign beauty.

Aimé Césaire

SEVENTH AND FINAL PROPOSITION

The poetically beautiful is not merely beauty of expression or muscular euphoria. A too Apollonian or gymnastic idea of beauty paradoxically runs the risk of skinning, stuffing, and hardening it.

COROLLARY

The music of poetry cannot be external or formal. The only *acceptable* poetic music comes from a greater distance than sound. To seek to musicalize poetry is the crime against poetic music, which can only be the striking of the mental wave against the rock of the world.

The poet is that very ancient yet new being, at once very complex and very simple, who at the limit of dream and reality, of day and night, between absence and presence, searches for and receives in the sudden triggering of inner cataclysms the password of connivance and power.

(1944–45)

translated by A. James Arnold

Lyric and Dramatic Poetry
1946–82

And the Dogs Were Silent

ACT 1

ECHO: For sure the Rebel is going to die. Oh, there will be no flags, not even black ones, no gun salutes, no ceremony. It will be very simple, something which in appearance will not change anything, but which will cause coral in the depths of the sea, birds in the depths of the sky, stars in the depths of women's eyes to crackle for the instant of a tear or the bat of an eyelash.

For sure the Rebel is going to die, the best reason being that there is nothing more to do in this crippled world: upheld and a prisoner of itself . . . he is going to die as it is written implicitly in wind and in sand by the hooves of wild horses and the loopings of rivers . . .

Fair game for the morgue, it is not tears which befit you, but the hawks of my fists and my flintlike thoughts, my silent invocation to the gods of disaster

Blue-eyed architect
I defy you

beware architect, for if the Rebel dies it will not be without making everyone aware that you are the constructor of a pestilential world
architect beware

who crowned you? During what night did you exchange compass for dagger?

architect deaf to things, as distinct as a tree but as closed as
   armor, each of your steps is a conquest and a spoliation
   and a misconception and an assassination

For sure the Rebel's going to leave the world, your world of
   rape in which the victim, thanks to you, is an unbaptized
   brute

architect gateless and starless Orcus without source without
   orient
architect with a peacock tail a crab scuttle words the blue of
   mushrooms and steel, beware

> *The curtain is raised.*
> *In the barathrum of terror, a vast*
> *collective jail, peopled with black*
> *candidates for madness and death;*
> *day thirty of famine, torture, and*
> *delirium.*
> *Silence.*

NARRATRESS: Go back home young women; play time is
   over; death's orbits thrust fulgurating eyes through the
   pale mica.

FIRST MADWOMAN, *seriously:* Is that a riddle?

NARRATOR: The season of burning stars is now at hand.

SECOND MADWOMAN, *laughing:* Ah, a story.

CHORUS, *threateningly:* The island stiffens its venomous
   spider legs over the muck of the barracoons.

FIRST MADWOMAN: Hou, hou.

SECOND MADWOMAN: Hou, hou.

NARRATOR: Young women, have some respect for the
   strangers walking in the sumptuous ruts of dusk.

> *The women step aside.*

And the Dogs Were Silent

ADMINISTRATOR: And they say we have stolen this land from them?
Ah! No! We took it
and that is not the same thing!
From whom?
From no one!
God gave it to us . . .
In fact, how could God tolerate, amidst the eddies of universal energy, this monstrous repose, this prodigious settling, this I dare say provocative deterioration prostrating itself.
Yes we took it
Oh! Not for us! For everyone!
In order to restore it, untimely stagnation that it is, to universal movement!
And in order that everyone may enjoy it,
like a scrupulous farmer,
like a loyal steward, we will keep it.

He sits down heavily.

Ungrateful people!
Moreover it is debatable whether there is in the world apart from ourselves any people who think, I mean really think, who do not ruminate the confused mingling of a few vapid ideas brought back to the lower brain still warm from their breathing or their sleep.

Wearily.

Ah we are alone
And what a burden!
To bear alone the burden of civilization!

He gets up. Paces up and down the veranda.

And who without us would take the census of nations and keep an accounting of the world?
And see how thanks to us the law, taking over the legacy of unclean instinct, dedicates it to Man.

Aimé Césaire

LOVER: Embrace me: life is *right here,* out of its own tatters the banana tree polishes its violet sex; dust sparkles, it is the fur of the sun, a splash of red leaves, it is the mane of the forest . . . my life is surrounded by threats of life, by promises of life.

REBEL: O death in which hunger ceases to gnaw, o soft bite, two black children on your doorsill are without parents, fat death, two skinny children holding hands on your door sill are crepuscular and barely alive.

LOVER: O sea, o undertow, o herd of flames full of fury, kick up your seed!

REBEL: O death, two black children in your sun, be peaceful and warm to them, o death, devourer of pigment, great equalizer, great just one without cop or sheriff, great encircler, great luller of brothers.

LOVER: Embrace me, this hour is beautiful; what is beauty if not this full weight of menace that the innocent batting of eyelash mesmerizes and lures into impotence? . . .

REBEL: What is beauty if not the torn poster of a smile on the thunderstruck door of a face? What is dying if not the stony face of discovery, the voyage outside of weeks and colors to the other side of the sun?

LOVER: Don't slander the sun. Do you see me cursing shadows? I worship you, shadow, fisher of the beautiful thick-haired screams of the sun, in your uncertain rivulets o the wind and its lingering gold washer fingers.

REBEL: O death, o queen, o strong-armed weaver, o carder, o cold unnumbed fingers, here we are before you the two of us rasping and knock-kneed across your warp—toward simple silence hurl your shuttle of sumptuous verse.

LOVER: My fair dear love, without us will the ungrateful sky swarm with open-eyed hawks,
without us will pearl oysters appease the sinuosity of the

And the Dogs Were Silent

secret wound with long sleepy gestures under the cover of
time?

my fair dear love, without us will the wind go forth deflower-
ing, moaning toward the arched awaiting?

REBEL: The mandrake perfume has evaporated; the hill is
dragging its hawsers; the great eddies of the valleys are
making waves; forests are losing their masts, birds are
sending distress signals from where our lost bodies are
rocking their whitened wreckage.

CHORUS: Who is the late one, the one who withers in
oblivescence?

SEMICHORUS: Stone of sulphur fallen from the clouds.

SEMICHORUS: Beautiful arch.

CHORUS: Beautiful blood.

SEMICHORUS: Beautiful rain.

SEMICHORUS: Seductress, oh . . .

CHORUS: Seductress, oh, I cannot chase from my eyes that
image: women eating dirt in a clay field.

SEMICHORUS: All the bronzings and all the hope on the
backs of their hands, in the palms of the hands of star
apple leaves will not console me.

REBEL: I captured extraordinary messages from space . . .
full of daggers, nights, and cries; I hear louder than praise
a vast improvisation of tornados, of sunstrokes, of evil
spells, of stones brewing strange dawns, the torpor im-
bibed sip by sip.

LOVER: A fearless bird is flinging its cry of young flame into
the warm belly of night.

REBEL: A great blaze of wild red plums and crabs . . .

A sowing (why not?) of flies, of palavers, of bad memories, of
termite trails, of fevers to be cooled, wrongs to be rec-
tified, an alligator yawn, an immense injustice.

Aimé Césaire

FIRST MADWOMAN: The dead are saluting the hired mourners.

SECOND MADWOMAN: I have heard death's skinny dog in the thunder . . .
Hail skinny companion.

Funeral music.

REBEL: Oh, my friends, enough: now I am merely fodder; sharks play in my wake.

CHORUS: The whites are landing, the whites are landing.

REBEL: The whites are landing. They're killing our daughters, comrades.

CHORUS, *terrified:* The whites are landing. The whites are landing.

SEMICHORUS: Spring forth, tears.

SEMICHORUS: Flow forth, dew.

REBEL: What do you see?

LOVER: Poto-poto life, a lot of mud.   *

CHORUS: Do you remember?

LOVER: Tree ferns . . . the torrential roar of water.

REBEL: The pitons, the coves . . . the rain . . . its pitch apple   *
arils . . .

LOVER: Oh! a landscape of laburnums, lakes, and bull-rushes and golden rain on rusty tin roofs.

REBEL: Canna roses, extinguish yourselves;
low water marks, be my sister.

The bishops enter, passing under the archbishop's crozier.

FIRST BISHOP: What an epoch: my children, a nice mess you've made of all this.

* Asterisks refer to terms glossed in the Translators' Notes.

And the Dogs Were Silent

He sits down on his throne.

SECOND BISHOP: An astonishing epoch, my brethren: the Newfoundland haddock volunteers to throw itself to our lines.

He sits down on his throne.

THIRD BISHOP: I say this is a dizzying or stupifying epoch, take your choice.

He sits down on his throne.

FOURTH BISHOP: A phallic epoch, fertile in miracles.

> *He laughs idiotically and sits down on his throne. The first three bishops tap their foreheads with their fingers and point at the fourth bishop to indicate that he is crazy.*

ARCHBISHOP: Let's go, I like animals with gorgeous coats; don't kill the cats.
ouha brrouha ou-ou-ah.

> *The bishops tap their foreheads with their fingers and point at the archbishop to indicate that he is out of his mind.*

ARCHBISHOP: Let's go, I hear the toad's pearly flute and the raspy screech of night crickets. Ouha bruhah.

> *The bishops rise, the group exits slowly.*
>
> *View of a forest and brambles. Black horsemen.*

FIRST HORSEMAN: Stuttering ferns, guide us.

SECOND HORSEMAN: Dried words of grass, guide us.

Aimé Césaire

THIRD HORSEMAN: Sore grass snakes, guide us.

FOURTH HORSEMAN: Fireflies, cries of flint, guide us.

FIFTH HORSEMAN: Guide us, o guide us, blind aloes, thundering vengeance armed for a century.

> *The group rides off, the horsemen disappear into the forest.*

FIRST MADWOMAN: Strange the way the evening walks its witches . . .

SECOND MADWOMAN: Looking like Popes, the egg-bellied spiders enter their thread palaces hailed by termites; in caverns yearning for sleep the lips of sharks quiver dreaming of hunts and carcasses. The safety nets of course no longer function: on the sea wall against the tide the cephalopods knitting their arms in a paroxysm of smelt wait and shout; marshes marshes, vomit forth your grass snakes.

NARRATRESS: Death gently cries in the neck of the soft wind.

NARRATOR: Fire hooks its rapacious haulms to the mesmerized housetops.

NARRATRESS: . . . the town collapses on its hams . . . in the slow vertigo of rape . . . amidst the ticklings in a bed of smoke and screams.

FIRST MADWOMAN: Women pass by jabbing out their fingernails . . . their words are terror . . . Oh, I hear the spelt of the night growing . . . women . . . the ditch is filled with blood . . . fire flakes are falling . . . I see lizards of fire, grasshoppers of fire, cush-cushes of fire.

REBEL: Don't talk this way. Don't talk this way . . . I am sitting in the devastation. My court, a pile of bones, my throne, rotting flesh, my crown, a circle of excrement. And look: strange nuptials have begun: ravens are the

And the Dogs Were Silent

rebec players, the bones, knucklebones; the puddles of wine on the ground are turning into fraternal clots where recumbent drunks remain for a long time . . . a long time.

NARRATRESS, *languishingly:* The moment has come when the weary princess wipes an absence of kisses from her lips as she would the thought of a bitter fruit.

> *She advances the hand halfway*
> *around the dial.*

The moment has come when the princess has ceased to believe in the hairy rainmaker.

> *She advances the hand halfway*
> *around the dial.*

The moment has come when wisp of smile by wisp of smile the princess weaves an unprecedented rain gown for herself.

> *She advances the hand halfway*
> *around the dial.*

NARRATRESS: The moment has come when . . .

GREAT PROMOTER: Come on! enough nonsense. The moment has come when we must assemble these Gentlemen. Let's proceed! The Admiral . . . the Troop Commander . . . the High Commissioner . . . the Surveyor . . . the Geometrician . . . the Judge . . . the Great Benedictorian . . . the Super Jailer . . . I almost forgot . . . the Banker.

> *Various responses are heard echoing*
> *in the corridor: "Here," "here we*
> *are" . . . "all right" . . .*

GREAT PROMOTER: Excellent! Everybody's here. We'll be able to work.

> *He advances the hand halfway*
> *around the dial.*

Aimé Césaire

Warm up the engine!

*The muffled sound of an engine puff-
ing louder and louder can be heard.*

GREAT PROMOTER:

As if reciting cabalistic formulas.

Track down, track down
throughout the lands, the seas, the air, wind up, wind up,
squeeze, squeeze. . . . There . . . steady!
Let no clod of earth remain untrampled, undug, uncultivated.
Squeeze, squeeze. . . .
Let the earth groan until it breaks in our virile embrace.
Knock down the fences, smash the idols, make all those bi-
    zarre names, those ill-planned faces vanish under our
    breath!
Ah! Gentlemen! Here we are! The world is caught in our net.
Ah ah ha! trample, trample!
They call me Greed, Greedy as they say!
How could we leave them to their dancing?
My name is Discoverer, my name is Inventor, my name is Uni-
    fier, the one who opens the world to nations!
Look: I extend my dexter
        I extend my sinister
        I put forth my right foot
        I put forth my left foot
                Ah! Well do I know
Freedom . . . their freedom . . .
And they think they're stopping me by throwing hollow word
    obstacles on my path.
But in spite of their asinine nicknames all of Mankind is
    sweating, searching, struggling, thinking,
But I ask you, are they, while . . .

He laughs.

A lovely calling card indeed!
These "Gentlemen" would be the Dancers of Mankind!
Enough of this crap!

And the Dogs Were Silent

I am the Expropriator.
I expropriate for reasons of eminent domain.
Let's go, gentlemen! To your stations!
Warm up the engine!
I'll crush all those who attempt to slow my advance.
I am History on the march!

NARRATOR: The moment has come when on the flaming
    threshold the princess calls a favorite cockatoo
cacatou
cacatou
in the empty book of neat defunct tillings.
The moment has come when, conjured by the cursing of souls,
    nine scorpions sting each other.

NARRATOR: The moment has come when a volcano scuttles
    itself in the coral bunker.
The moment has come when the empress decrees the useless-
    ness of equalization funds in the grottoes of the empire
    and tattoos her thighs with a shower of daturas in which
    a flambé sword is rattling.

NARRATRESS, *solemnly:* An arpeggio of sinister guitars,
    there rises under my eyelids
a dawn bled to death—
I am an awaiting—nothing but an awaiting.
I tread on the thin ice of precious moments,
O the fragile stubborn and sure paths of my kingdom which is
    and is not yet . . .
The weather is fair monstrously fair.
Surge forth, you weeks, you scruples of dying worlds;
surge forth, pregnant girls;
foam against my scandalous waiting.

NARRATOR, *humbly:* Here I am, a man, an empty-handed
    merchant, my naked eye eliciting the spectacle, my throat
    churning the living words hatched against my teeth.

NARRATRESS: Here I am, I, I: a woman obsessed by big
    words—toward the elementary smell of cadavers I swim
    amidst gladiolas and Jericho roses.

Aimé Césaire

REBEL: That's not true . . . there are no more battles. No more murders, right? No more flamboyant crimes? Blindly the street organ drones out minutes of silence, shavings of dustless time.
Ho, Ho, the smell of cadavers . . . blood bubbling like a fat barrel of wine.

NARRATRESS: All it takes is a knock on the sun's window-pane. One only needs to break the sun's plate glass. One only needs to discover in the sun's box the red crests of venomous ants bursting in every direction. Ha. Ha.

NARRATOR: Splendid weather. A gerbera more naked than a woman in the sun is turning toward the sun and the sun crackles in closed brains a mined tiara, a traveler's tree, a braided heart, gorgeous high-blown-frozen-waters.

FIRST MADWOMAN: The smell of earth hacked open by machetes of fine rain. The simple day is a dumping ground for the dying . . . Oh, I push aside the leaves of noise. Oh, I listen through the cracks in my brain. It rises. It rises . . .

SECOND MADWOMAN: It rises. It rises. The sun is a maddened lion dragging himself, paws broken, around the shuddering cage.

REBEL, *feverishly:* It rises . . . it rises from the depths of the earth . . . the black flood rises . . . waves of howling . . . marshes of animal smells . . . the storm frothy with human feet . . . and still more are pouring in a swarm down paths of the mornes, climbing the escarpments of ravines, obscene and savage torrents swollen with chaotic streams, rotted seas, convulsive oceans, in the coal-black laughter of cutlasses and cheap booze . . .

FIRST MADWOMAN: In my red and black hand the dawn of a white alder is breathless.

SECOND MADWOMAN: In the beginning there was nothing.

REBEL, *softly:* Night and misery, comrades, misery and animal resignation, the night rustling with the breathing of

And the Dogs Were Silent

slaves dilating under their Christophoric steps the great   *
sea of misery, the great sea of black blood, the great swell
of sugarcane and dividends, the great ocean of horror and
desolation. In the end, there is the end . . .

> *He covers his eyes.*
>
> *Far, very far, in a historical dis-
> tance—while the chorus mimes a
> scene of black rebellion—monoto-
> nous and barbaric songs, confused
> tramping, cutlasses and pikes, the
> speaker—a grotesque nigger—ges-
> ticulates. The whole thing is sinister
> and clownish, reeking of pomposity
> and cruelty.*

SPEAKER: Silence, gentlemen, silence.

FIRST ENERGUMEN: Don't talk to us about silence: we are
free and equal in rights. Don't you forget it.

SECOND ENERGUMEN: And I say: a curse upon those who
have not read the Mene, Mene, Tekel, Upharsin of tyr-
anny inscribed on the walls of our honorable faces freed
from the halter.
And now, I know of heads that will roll like cocoa pods: death
to the whites.

CHORUS OF ENERGUMENS: Death to the whites, death to
the whites.

> *Reverberating echoes, vociferations,
> chants. Emptiness and silence re-
> sume, heavily.*

NARRATRESS, *in a slashing voice:* In the end . . . what I see
in the end . . . Ah, yes . . . at the very end . . . the collapse
of the beast, chomping ghouls landing on this hysterical
shit, its benumbing haunted by terror, its insolence
chewed up with prayers, and on its wounds the pimento
sauce of my laughter and the salt of my tears.

NARRATOR: Islands, I love this cool word watched over by Caribs and sharks.

NARRATRESS: Oh I am passionately waiting: I am surrounded . . .

NARRATOR: . . . surrounded by nightmarish eyes . . .

NARRATRESS: . . . surrounded by children and by eyes and by bursts of laughter.

NARRATOR: Cataracts; here come the cataracts, and the keen murderous song of birds.

NARRATRESS, *throwing down her mask:* Beware, I shout beware from the height of my watchtower
closer
over here
with my sweet and slow voice of meager harvests and unexpected rain
the black cloud is forming a slipknot.

NARRATOR, *throwing down his mask:* Beware, I shout beware from the height of my watchtower
closer
over here
the freebooters' dingy on a blue field: in order to amuse themselves.
Drunkenness and debauchery. An immense expanse turns gold;
in the depths of the lake a vermeil eagle is bathing;
fields of maize, of indigo, of sugarcane, a few fathoms below;
in the hollow, uproars rush to the hollow and plug the sky . . .

CHORUS, *singing:* Hé, my friends, Ho.

SECOND CHORISTER, *singing:* Hé, my friends, Ho.

FIRST CHORISTER: The earth is a weariness; my weariness will weary it.

SECOND CHORISTER: The sun is a weariness; my weariness will weary it.

And the Dogs Were Silent

THIRD CHORISTER: Rain is a weariness; my weariness will weary it.

FIRST CHORISTER: Hé, my friends, Ho.

SECOND CHORISTER: My weariness is an abyss; no sleep could possibly fill it.

THIRD CHORISTER: My weariness is a thirst. . . . Ho, no drink could quench it.

CHORUS: Hé, Ho, my friends, Ho. My weariness is a loaded cart of noiseless sand in the four corners of petrified harvests.

FIRST MADWOMAN, *singing:* Where is the one who will sing for us?

CHORUS: He holds a snake in his right hand,
in his left a mint leaf,
his eyes are sparrow hawks, his head a dog's head.

SECOND MADWOMAN, *singing:* Where is the one who will show us the road?

CHORUS: His sandals are of pale sun,
the straps of fresh blood.

FIRST MADWOMAN, *singing:* Let us prepare the house for the triumphant and handsome guest.

SECOND MADWOMAN, *singing:* O dogs, o scorpions, o snakes, only steps, true steps that rise from the shadows.

SECOND MADWOMAN, *singing:* Let us prepare the path for the charged and handsome man.

CHORUS, *clapping their hands:* In vain does the last of the living hide.
To praise him we do not need tambourines,
manioc from burnt lands, camp fires, holà! listen to me, I am thirsty for your incendiary arrows, for your red pepper fumes, for your genip, your curare.
To praise and to encourage him we do not need tambourines,

Aimé Césaire

holà, in the blood, sustained fire, start the fire in the shadow
and the trench,
a thousand apologies, that's the most we can offer you: a
flickering fire panting salutes to the obscurity armed with
blue shadows.

FIRST MADWOMAN: I shall lay him between my breasts
like a mint leaf,
I shall lay him between my breasts like a stick of incense,
I shall lay him between my breasts like a red dagger.

CHORUS, *chanting:* With your sandals of rain and courage,
ascend, appear, imminent
lord, so close to tears, come up in the desert like water, like
the rise of waters swelling with corpses and crops;
ascend, most imminent lord, flesh whirls in the shavings of
dark Africa, ascend most imminent lord, there will still
be eyes like sunflowers or tall amorous soybeans, flocks
of birds as beautiful as the bugle call of an Adam's apple
in the lightning of flashing angers.

NARRATRESS: You heard, you heard, the king is arriving,
the king is landing; the king is ascending the staircase;
the king is stepping up over the first step; he is reaching
the second; the king is on the perron.

NARRATOR, *very calmly:* Step by step the king placed his
foot into the trench camouflaged with slippery smiles.

REBEL: You will not stop me from talking to my friends
without eclipse,
plump moon malefic weed, sycamore sycamore . . .
here are my loves, here are my hatreds
and my voice a perfect child at your alcove's edge.

CHORUS, *from a distance:* Rise, O King.

REBEL: The river without idiom resents the maneuvers of
the ash
the cape and the filing

And the Dogs Were Silent

the birds and the days
revolve with their clangings of locks;
on the infant horizon fabulous beasts
—grazers of brains—
have put away their eyes
delighted at having drunk all of the night.

CHORUS, *from a distance:* Rise, O King.

REBEL: I want to populate the night with meticulous farewells.

CHORUS, *distantly:* Rise, O King.

REBEL: Violets anemones are springing up with each step of my blood . . .

CHORUS, *farther away:* Rise, O King.

REBEL: . . . with each step of my voice, with each drop of my name . . .

CHORUS, *even farther away:* Rise, O King.

REBEL: . . . arucaria cones, bunches of cherries . . .

CHORUS, *practically lost in the distance:* Rise, O King.

REBEL, *in a thundering voice:* . . . arches, signs, prints, fires. . . .

CHORUS, *groaning:* Rise, O King.

REBEL: I had brought this land to the knowledge of itself,
acquainted this land with its own secret demons,
lit up in craters of heloderms and cymbals
the symphonies of an unknown hell, splendidly parasitized with haughty nostalgias.

CHORUS: Rise, O King.

REBEL: And now
alone
everything is alone

no matter how I sharpen my voice
all deserts all
my voice labors
my voice pitches in the foghorn of mists without crossroad
and I have no mother
and I have no sons.

CHORUS: Rise, O King.

REBEL: I understand. Holà, galley slave back off, your part
is finished.
Beautiful as when memory relinquishes recent oblivion, ven-
geance rises with the day's ear and all the dust that weaves
the flesh of night, all the wasps that salivate the cassava of
night, all the barracudas that scrawl graffiti on the back
of night, press on until glimpsing their eye of youth.
Behold I now salute the last night of my sex
hearth
ember
sun rooted in the mines of my strength
you will not frighten me ghosts, I am strong.
I have muzzled the sea while listening to gardeners struggle to-
ward the fabulous rump of morning in a softness of scan-
dal and spume.

The light goes out.

REBEL: I have a pact with this night, for the last twenty years
I have felt it softly hail me . . .

A flickering of candlelight.

REBEL: I hailed my gods by dint of disowning them . . .

Sneers.

but they are watching me, spying me out, and I'm scared
—evil and jealous gods—
and their arms are long, vast, and their hands are webbed.
No way out
I'm saying I've had it

And the Dogs Were Silent

I'm saying I cannot
How shall I make them understand that I do not want. That I
    cannot
Not a clump of sleep, nor a clump of silence that does not hide
    a god
and voices say that I am a traitor, I am not an ingrate
I prostrate myself, lower my head
and a kid bleats in my heart.

> *He stops. Grimacing frozen faces ap-*
> *pear: they are fetishes: fabulous*
> *beasts, deformed faces, enormous*
> *white pupils.*

REBEL, *flat on his belly:* Here I am . . .

> *Pause.*

no matter how white one paints the base of the tree, the
    strength of the bark screams underneath . . .

> *Pause.*

why would I fear the judgment of my gods?
who said I was a traitor?

> *Pause.*

the strange beggars with millennial faces who sometimes
    threaten
sometimes salute the dawn
they're me
every night a hunger awakens them amidst the madrepores
a hunger for a larger sun and very ancient coins.
I face again towards the unknown wind humped by pursuits.
I'm leaving
do not speak, do not laugh
Africa is asleep, do not speak, do not laugh. Africa is bleeding,
    my mother,
Africa, shattered, is opening herself to a ditch of vermin,
to a sterile invasion of the spermatozoa of rape.

FIRST TEMPTER'S VOICE: What thread stretched across
   the forests the rivers the marshes the tongues and the
   wild beasts?
I have no mother I have no past
I have filled in the unmotherly shaft of my navel to the point of
   forgetting the dust and the insults.

REBEL: Step back, torturers
ah you wink at me
you insist on my complicity?
Help, help, murder!
They've killed the sun there's no more sun, all that's left are
   Bashan's bulls
torches attached to their furious tails
assassins, assassins!
That's it . . . they've sniffed out nigger flesh—
they're stopping
they're laughing.

SECOND TEMPTER'S VOICE: It's over, it's all over, no
   point in filing a complaint, judicial function is finished.
Look, they've torn him to pieces, to pieces like a wild pig,
like an agouti! like a mongoose!
Who did that? You ask me who did that?
No it was not me
I am innocent
Who?
They
they the dogs
they the men with bloody lips, with steel eyes but you know
   what I am telling you: judicial function is finished.
Finished, but the gleam in their eyes is never quenched.
Assassins, assassins, assassins!

REBEL, *stepping into the barathrum and going from corpse
   to corpse:* The ash, the dream . . . famished, famished;
two hands burning on the plate of the sun . . .
O you dead . . . and the master's sadism and the slave's death

And the Dogs Were Silent

rattle under the coprophagic violence completes in lines
of vomit the shark's yapping and the scolopendra's crawl.
O, you who have died in a free land.
The beautiful blind eyes of the earth spontaneously sing
hooky playing, the joined eyebrows of plowed highlands, the
crafty
maneuvers of idiotic conversations in the quicksand. The
shipwrecker's cow, the rain of calvaries and waves, are   *
bewitching with snakes of palavering kelp the lighthouse
cut off from blood and shadow.
O you dead without cavessons.
With sky, with birds, with parrots, bells, bandanas, drums,
airy smoke, furious caresses, copper tones, mother-of-
pearl, Sundays, dance halls, childrens' words, words of
love,
with love, with childrens' mittens,
I shall build a world our world
my round-shouldered world
of wind of sun of moon of rain of full moon
a world of little spoons
of velvet
of gold lamé
of peaks of valleys of petals of cries of a frightened fawn
some day
long ago
equal sisters will take each others' hands in the torture chambers
the world will very gently bend its crooked head in order
to die
the days neatly lined up like an orphanage going to mass
the days with their demeanors of polite assassins will disrobe
themselves of milk of grass of hours
with their demeanor of wild cherry trees
with their slave-ship politeness on the route of swans
with their looks of famous castles
but with unknown halls as beautiful as the lie that is nothing
else than love for the journey some day long ago, truce of

god without god, harbors unknown forever, suns unknown forever.

SEMICHORUS: Man, beware . . .

The lover steps forward . . .

ACT   2

NARRATOR: And now, here comes the black boatman of the
   black storm, the watchman
of black weather and of rainy luck—
walled up in the black passion of a black voyage
all he's aware of is the storm,
a stubborn old man, frail, a black interrogation of fate in
   the lost
cycle of summary currents
but his battle is with winds and rocks
not with his sex and his heart . . .

REBEL: Get away I am just a defeated man
back off
All I am is someone severed
offered and rejected
I dedicate myself to the absolute wind
I a defeated harvester of tepid flesh
exalted by the invigorating triumph of seagulls.

Pause.

Do you know Wagadugu, the city of dried mud?

CHORUS: Don't talk like that!

REBEL: Do you know Jenne, the red city?

CHORUS: O don't talk like that!

REBEL: Do you know Timbuktu?

CHORUS: Don't talk, don't even speak . . .

Aimé Césaire

REBEL: I have spread my scarf across the waters, across the
    waters of death.
I have spread my scarf, hé.
Lend me a parasol for the Wagadugu sun.

Pause.

Because I have pulled all night against my chain
because the links from so much yapping had dug into my
    black and twitching flesh
the minutes parade around me
like a pack of emaciated wolves
like a herd of lashing whips
like the knots of a ladder of statutes and rope.
Rebellious subject perfect victim
a challenge riveted to the foreheads of ponds
I do not converse with the gods
I do not heal the possessed
Why wait to spit on me
the thick spittle of centuries,
ripened
over 306 years
Too late it's too late
my friends I'm not home for anyone
for anyone
except for a flood too diluted to glint with stars
except for mud with burned eyes burned sex
Through my eyes buffeted by alfalfa, girls are racing
sounding their river clogs
their dustless arboreal voices
their slender torsos of bread, of plains,
and look
I ordered for my funeral
a herd of wild buffalo
one hundred eunuchs sacrifices tumults
a flight of throwing-knives of red copper assegais
My body my body
a stretcher, I will not fling the wounded one to the dogs of the
    hawthorn.

And the Dogs Were Silent

The moon rises.

REBEL: rotten moon
her lover his lover
the fetish tree
her lover his lover
the hill is a big pail of water that does not cease spilling in the
    light of volcanic faults
of eyelashes
of lands
the sky demanded fingerprints from the frangipani
end of worlds of numbers
naturally they lied I wasn't there
at the adoration of the magi; the only thing working for me is
    my word
by the grace of young lands and the seismic basin
and of flowered marshes on the face of a wound
phoenix glowworm catalpa clear light
my word the power of fire
my word breaking the cheeks of tombs of ashes of lanterns
my word that no chemistry could ever tame or encompass
milky hands without words without loincloth—dragon of
    the thaw
my great desire barbaric naked black sagacious and brown.

Pause.

Ho ho
Their power is firmly anchored
Acquired
Required
My hands bathe in heaths of clairin. In rice fields of roucou.   *
And I have my calabash of pregnant stars. But I am weak. Oh
    I am weak.
Help me.
And here I find myself again in the rush of metamorphosis
drowned blinded
afraid of myself, frightened by myself. . . .
Gods . . . you are not gods. I am free.

Aimé Césaire

Your voices merely boomerang back the stone of my own voice.
Your eyes merely envelope me in my own flames.
Your throwing-knives whistling around my head leap
from the cactus patch of my poisoned blood
Never mind. The willows are forming prairies of rusty crotons
Poinsettias encircle me and disgorge the red
dagger of memory
in the bile of their leaves
and now girls are joining in
here come the fire girls
the chanterelles of hell
red satin butterflies with wings more sonorous than speech or
    night
their buttocks sweep the night with their floodlights
flamethrowers set fire to the scrub of their breasts
of their loins
of their thighs of brown milk black honey red honey
Hé ho papa love
light the fire
light the fire of your red limbs
of your red hair your red feet
set the reddened bank on fire with your reddened sex
bombaïa
bombaïa

                              *

He faints.

SEMICHORUS: His back is up against the days.

SEMICHORUS: His back is up against the night.

SEMICHORUS: I recall the evenings, dusk was a blue-green
    hummingbird climaxing in the red hibiscus.

SEMICHORUS: Dusk hesitated shivering and frail amidst
    scrap-iron-mending locusts.

NARRATRESS: Let him sleep.

NARRATOR: Let him sleep.

CHORUS: Mornes, tunics with river-girded loins.

And the Dogs Were Silent

NARRATRESS: Let him sleep.

NARRATOR: Let him sleep.

CHORUS: April mango trees, drawn swords, islands.

NARRATOR: Let him ripen in the beautiful pod of sleep.

NARRATRESS: Let him sleep.
In his sleep there are islands, islands like the sun, islands like
   a long bread loaf on the water, islands like women's
   breasts, islands like well-made beds, islands warm as
   hands, islands lined with champagne and women . . . Ah,
   let him sleep . . . sleep . . .

REBEL, *trying to get up:* And let me scream, let me scream
   the good drunk scream of revolt to my heart's content, I
   want to be alone in my skin,
I do not grant anyone the right to inhabit me,
haven't I the right to be alone between the walls of my bones?
and I protest and I don't want a guest—it's awful—
I can't take a step without being seized.
In the ravine, on the mountain, in the bayahonde, chewing on   *
   sugarcane, sucking on ciruelas . . .
The statue that we are erecting, comrades, the most beautiful
   of statues. It is for absolute hearts, across its arms our
   terrible despair from so much trembling, in an air heavy
   and emptied of birds, the most beautiful of statues, the
   only one from which nettles do not sprout: solitude.

SECOND MADWOMAN: Quiet! dog; die then—enough,
   enough!

He collapses again.

NARRATRESS: Let him sleep! Let the sandy porpoises emerge
   between the high shards of storm toward the young and
   cavalier foam. . . .

NARRATOR, *confidentially:* Did I dream it up? It was a re-
   nowned city paved with frolicking dolphins and raffia
   apples whose tender breasts registered the slightest droop-
   ings of love. . . .

Aimé Césaire

NARRATRESS: Oh, I never dreamed . . . and the air is lighter. And the noise will come to me deafened by many centuries. And I will gather it on my breast of silence until this beautiful fish gasping from its luxuriating agony of a creature more golden and smoother than all other creatures arrives thrashing at my feet . . . vengeance. . . .

CHORUS: I am the sacred tambourine player, one who in tentative light and musty odors confidently strikes his ligneous palm and mallet, the king of dawn and of gods, the redheaded fisherman of things profound and black.

SEMICHORUS, *distractedly:* . . . a sunspot of ripe gold and rose on the skin of the water.

SEMICHORUS, *distractedly:* Ho, ho, there was a salmon-colored bougainvillea and the tall clear grey of a palmtree the constrictor embrace of a liana gorged with blue venom.

CHORUS: A just dawn minted a smile.
A just dawn minted hope.
A just dawn minted simple words ringing clearer than plowshares . . .
for us it is always a season of rain
and of venomous beasts
and of women who collapse pregnant from having hoped . . .

CHORUS: Have you risen?

REBEL: I have risen.

CHORUS: Have you risen in a proper way?

REBEL: In a proper way.

REBEL: And it is true; it is a thousand times true hail dead leaf.

REBEL: World, beware, there is a beautiful country that they have spoiled with dissolute unseasonable larvae
a world of shattered flowers dirtied with old posters

And the Dogs Were Silent

a house of broken tiles of leaves torn apart without a tempest
not yet
not yet
I will only come back in dignity
love will shine in our eyes of a burning barn like a drunken
    bird
a firing squad
not yet
not yet
I will only come back with a good load of booty
grassy vibrant love of wheat of grasshoppers of waves of
    floods of whistling of glowing fires of signs of forests of
    water of lawns of water of herds of water
spacious love of flames, of instants, of beehives, of peonies, of
    poinsettias, prophetic in number, prophetic in climates.

CHORUS: Hatchets my sweet canticles
spilled blood my warm fur
massacres, my massacres, the smoke, my smoke forms an
    opaque road of water jets spurting from fireplugs.

REBEL: Plow me, plow me, armed cry of my people; plow
    me
warthog and trample trample me
until my heart breaks
until my veins burst
until my bones chirp in the midnight of my flesh . . .

FIRST TEMPTER'S VOICE: I am the red hour, the red un-
    knotted hour.

SECOND TEMPTER'S VOICE: I am the hour of nostalgias,
    the hour of miracles.

REBEL: O the sweetness in my hands when they build—
    never will creative hands have caressed so much adven-
    ture in the thing they are creating
and I keep ramming into the thick muzzle of the present the
    words "some day"
some day with the sun a thick-haired prairie in the sky

and there's not a single small cloud that my hand has not al-
ready stroked the fragile feathers of a bird trembling on
the edge of its nest.

> *In the distance one hears the cries of*
> *"Death to the whites."*

REBEL: Why did I say "Death to the whites?"
Do they think this savage cry pleases me?

> *He thinks.*

It is quite true that at this point in time
there are accounts to be drawn up.
How shall I put it? What words to use?
Were the deed copied by criminal hands
were it signed not with a seal of ink
but by a blood clot
still I would not try to escape the authority of the grimoire.

Resentment? No. I resent the injustice, but under no circum-
stances would I trade my place for that of the executioner
and give him small change for his bloody coin.

Rancor? No. To hate is to still be dependent.
What is hatred, if not the wood collar tied to the slave's neck
and that hampers him
or the awesome barking of the dog that sinks its teeth into his
throat
and I, I have refused, once and for all, to be a slave.
Oh! none of this is simple. This cry of "Death to the whites,"
not screaming it,
it is true, means accepting the fetid sterility of worn-out soil,
but ha!
not crying "Death" to this cry of "Death to the whites" in-
volves another poverty. For me,
I accept this cry only as the chemical in the fertilizer
whose sole worth is in that dying
that regenerates a land without pestilence, rich, delectable,
smelling not of fertilizer but of ceaselessly fresh grass.
How to disentangle all that?

And the Dogs Were Silent

Let's suppose the world is a forest. Fine!
There are baobabs, some live oaks, black firs, white wal-
　　nut trees;
I want all of them to grow, nicely firm and dense,
different in wood, in bearing, in color,
but equally rich in sap and without one encroaching upon
　　another,
different at their bases
but . . . oh!

　　　　　　　Ecstatically.

Let their tops join yes very high in the even ether that will
　　form a single roof
for all of them
I say a single tutelary roof!
My heart,
for long days I've ground grain between stones;
for long nights I've watched the fire stutter.
O sweetness, here comes the Aurora—
For every quarter
with my flayed hands
I attach the bridles of your red horses . . .

　　　　　　His lover rushes into the cell.

LOVER: My dearest!

　　　　　　*The rebel gently disengages himself
　　　　　　from her.*

REBEL: Too late it's too late
my love, I am not home for anyone
for anyone.

LOVER: If you ever loved me, if ever . . .

REBEL: When the obsidian wind sweeps by
why weigh it down with a violent word?

LOVER: Fate, I know, is a runaway horse
but perhaps a child's cry
your child's cry . . .

Aimé Césaire

REBEL: . . . born from my most impulsive blood
from the zenith of my love
replete with my ardor at its peak
I will feed him a great example.

LOVER: It is not examples
it is bread, care, sleepless nights he should be fed, yes warm
tenderness, trembling presence . . .

REBEL: And to achieve this?

LOVER: To achieve this you must live.

REBEL: Ah, yes, this life that all of you keep offering me:
Thank you.   Ah, that is what destroys all of you
and the country destroys itself by wanting at any cost to jus-
tify accepting the unacceptable.
I want to be the one who says no to the unacceptable.
In this compromised life I myself want to carve
a birdless monument of Refusal,
out of windswept dacite.

LOVER: The absolute, my absolute is life,
it's the sun, it's you. It's me, it's our child
eager to be, whom you sacrifice to your illusions.

REBEL: Illusions? When the sun is late,
do you doubt that it will rise?

LOVER: It rises every day.

REBEL: Ours does too . . . every day . . . each day step by step
it rises toward a zenith, reaching thousands of hearts.

LOVER: Words! Those are mere words!
Confess, you're playing at carving a beautiful death for your-
self, but
I am the one who cuts across your game and cries out!

REBEL: Woman, don't weaken me with quarrelsome speech,
today is a day for greatness, allow me great courage.

LOVER: You're pretending! But deep in yourself you know
full well that things will not change.

Will blood be less hesitant?
Will man ever be closer to the landscape than a tree?

REBEL: Obviously one can say so
obviously one must say so
but only afterwards!
In advance, it's a pretext!
And I do not approve of people giving themselves pretexts
in order to avoid a quest.
Enough!

LOVER: You see, you don't even have faith.
Only your pride
and it is to that god that you sacrifice!
With what light does he illuminate you?
What refreshing water does he provide you with?
Your god is nothing but the scrap of an idea
that habit has wedged into your stubborn brain.

REBEL: Please, be quiet.

LOVER: I will not be quiet
I do not grant myself the right
I will darken the night itself with the furious smoke of my
    screams, to make it unbreathable for the stubborn nostril.

REBEL: Dear one . . . my lover from difficult days,
be my friend in the last fight.
My son?
So, you will tell him about the great struggle,
three centuries of bitter night conspiring against us.
Tell him that I did not want this country to be nothing more
than fodder for the eye, the crude stuff of spectacle,
I mean this confused mass of hills cut across by fingers of
    water!

LOVER: Yes, you wanted it to be something else: a widow's
    screams,
an orphan's moaning!

Aimé Césaire

REBEL: Tell him,
how would I tell him?
Woman
how grateful these people will be to me I do not know
but I do know they needed something beyond a beginning
something like a birth.
Let my blood, yes, my blood
be the foundation of this people
and you . . .

LOVER: I should let you die?
Embrace me the world is young.

REBEL: O how fragile the world is.

LOVER: Embrace me: the air like baking bread turns gold
and rises.

REBEL: How solemn the world is!

LOVER: Embrace me: the world flows with aigrettes, with
spikenard umbels, with cassia desires.

REBEL: Oh the world resounds dully with rearing horses.

LOVER: Embrace me; embrace me; in my eyes worlds are
made and unmade; I hear the music of the spheres . . .
the horses approach . . . a bundle of shivers force-feeds
the carnal wind with venison . . .

A prodigious silence.

REBEL: Woman . . .

*The mother immobile until now
pushes the Lover aside.*

MOTHER: And the most unfortunate is still at your feet.

REBEL: At my feet? For a long time I have spoken only to
the one who causes the night to be alive and the day to
be leafy.

SEMICHORUS: The one who turns the morning into a stream
of blue junks?

And the Dogs Were Silent

SEMICHORUS: The one who makes . . .

REBEL: . . . the flint unforgiveable. Woman of the sunset,
    woman without encounters, what have we to say to each
    other? At the red hour of sharks, at the red hour of nostal-
    gias, at the red hour of miracles, I encountered *Freedom*.
And death was not cantankerous but sweet
with hands of Brazilian rosewood and of a young nubile girl
with hands of fonio and shredded linen   *
sweet
we were there
a hymen was bleeding that night
helmsman of the night populated with suns and rainbows
helmsman of the sea and of death
freedom o my gawky gal your legs sticky with fresh blood
your cry of a surprised bird, of a fascine
and of a shabeen in the depths of the water   *
of an alburnum and of a trial and of a triumphant litchi
and of a sacrilege
crawl crawl
my gawky one populated with horses and foliage
and with risks and with acquaintances
with heritage and with sources
at the peak of your loves at the peak of your delays
at the peak of your canticles
of your lanterns
on your insectlike and rootlike tips
crawl great drunken spawn of bulldogs of mastiffs of baby
    wild boards
of lanceolate pit vipers and of fires
in order to rout the scrofulous examples of poultices.

MOTHER: O my imperfectly hatched son.

REBEL: Who is the one who disturbs me on the threshold of
    repose? Ah, you needed a son who would be betrayed
    and sold . . . and you chose me . . . Thank you.

MOTHER: My son.

Aimé Césaire

REBEL: And those who sent you needed—isn't it true?—more than my defeat, more than my rupturing chest, they needed my *yes* . . . And they sent you. Thank you.

MOTHER: Turn around and look at me.

REBEL: Dear one, dear one,
is it my fault if in puffs from the depths of the ages, reddening faster than my fusc blackens, the shame of years, the red of years and the inclemency of days are rising in me, coloring and covering me
rainy days of shoddy goods
the insolence of grasshopper days
the barking of bulldog days whose muzzles are more glazed than salt
I am ready
resounding with all the noise and filled with confluences
I am stretching my black skin as if it were donkey skin.

MOTHER: Heart full of war, milkless heart.

REBEL: Faithless mother.

MOTHER: My child . . . give me your hand . . . let your hand simple once again grow in my hand.

REBEL: The tom-tom pants, the tom-tom burps, the tom-tom spits grasshoppers of fire and blood. My hand is also full of blood.

MOTHER, *frightened:* Your eyes are full of blood.

REBEL: I'm no arid heart. I'm not a merciless heart.
I am a man of good thirst, crazed, circling the poisoned ponds.

MOTHER: No . . . circling a salt desert, and not one star except the gibbet of mutineers and black limbs in the fangs of the wind.

REBEL, *sneering:* Ha, Ha, what a revenge for the whites. The indocile sea . . . the grimoire of signs . . . famine, despair . . . But no, they must have lied to you, and the sea is leafy, and from the height of its crest I am reading

And the Dogs Were Silent

a magnificent land, full of sun . . . of parrots . . . of fruit . . . of fresh water . . . of breadfruit trees . . .

MOTHER: . . . a desert of concrete, of camphor, of steel, of rags, of disinfected swamps,
a heavy place mined by eyes by flames and by mushrooms . . .

REBEL: A land of coves, of palm leaves, of screw pines . . . a land of open hands . . .

MOTHER: See, he doesn't obey . . . he's not renouncing his evil vengeance . . . he's not putting aside his anger.

REBEL, *toughly:* My family name: offended; my given name: humiliated; my profession: rebel; my age: the stone age.

MOTHER: My race: the human race. My religion: brother-hood . . .

REBEL: My race: the fallen race. My religion . . .
but it is not you who will prepare it with your disarmament; it is I with my revolt and my poor clenched fists and my bushy head.

Very calmly:

I recall a November day; he was not six months old and the master came into the shack murky as an April moon, and he was probing the child's small muscled limbs, he was a very good master, he ran his fat fingers caressingly across his little dimpled face. His blue eyes were laughing and his mouth was teasing him with sugary things: this one will make a good one, the master said looking at me, and   *
he was saying other friendly things, the master was, that you had to start very early, that twenty years were not too much to make a good Christian and a good slave, a good subject, utterly devoted, a good slavedriver for an over-seer, with a sharp eye and a strong arm. And this man was speculating over my son's cradle, a slave driver's cradle.

MOTHER: Alas you will die.

Aimé Césaire

REBEL: Killed . . . I killed him with my own hands . . .
Yes: a fecund and copious death . . .
it was night. We crawled through the sugarcane.
The cutlasses were chortling at the stars, but we didn't care
    about the stars.
The cane slashed our faces with streams of green blades
we crawled cutlass in fist . . .

MOTHER: I had dreamed of a son who would close his moth-
    er's eyes.

REBEL: I chose to open my child's eyes to another sun.

MOTHER: . . . O my son . . . an evil and pernicious death.

REBEL: Mother, a verdant and sumptuous death.

MOTHER: From too much hate.

REBEL: From too much love.

MOTHER: Spare me, I'm choking from your shackles, bleed-
    ing from your wounds.

REBEL: And the world does not spare me. There is not in the
    world one single poor lynched bastard, one poor tortured
    man, in whom I am not also murdered and humiliated.

MOTHER: God in heaven, deliver him!

REBEL: My heart, you will not deliver me of my memories . . .
It was a November night . . .
And suddenly clamors lit up the silence,
we had leapt, we the slaves, we the manure, we beasts with
    patient hooves.
We were running like lunatics; fiery shots broke out . . . We
    were striking. Sweat and blood cooled us off. We were
    striking admidst the screams and the screams became
    more strident and a great clamor rose toward the east,
    the outbuildings were burning and the flames sweetly
    splashed our cheeks.
Then came the attack on the master's house.
They were shooting from the windows.

And the Dogs Were Silent

We forced the doors.

The master's bedroom was wide open. The master's bedroom was brilliantly lit, and the master was there, very calm . . . and all of us stopped . . . he was the master . . . I entered. It's you, he said, very calmly . . . It was me, it was indeed me, I told him, the good slave, the faithful slave, the slave slave, and suddenly my eyes were two cockroaches frightened on a rainy day . . . I struck, the blood spurted: it is the only baptism that today I remember.

MOTHER: I am afraid of the bullets of your words, I am afraid of your words of pitch and ambush. I am afraid of your words because I cannot take them into my hands and weigh them . . . They are not human words.

They are not words one can take in the palms of one's hands and weigh on quivering scales lined with roads . . .

The mother collapses.

REBEL, *leaning over the dead or fainted one:* Woman, your face is more worn than a pumice stone tumbled along by a river

utterly, utterly,

your fingers are more fatigued than cane crushed by the mill, utterly, utterly,

Oh, your hands are crumpled bagasse, utterly, utterly,

Oh, your eyes are utterly lost stars, utterly,

Utterly worn down mother, leafless mother you are a flamboyant that now only bears pods. You are a calabash, and you are no more than a crop of couis . . .   *

Pause.

A VOICE: Assassin, he killed his master

A VOICE: Assassin—curse him—he is going to kill his mother.

A VOICE: Assassin, kill him, cut off his hands.

A VOICE: Kill him, kill him, gouge out his eyes.

A VOICE: That's it, let's gouge out his eyes.

Aimé Césaire

REBEL, *blinded:* Chargers of the night, take me away.

CHORUS: The day under contagious rain, a shut down house
The day in the poisoned night is a shut down city.
O convict, O pilgrim, under the rain and in the doorless night
your stooped steps, my stooped steps in the passageway with-
out hands and without ears without water and without
knocker tortured by sentries.

REBEL: Chargers of the night, take me away . . .

Stepping toward the chorus.

My children, I am a king who owns nothing.

CHORUS: Rise, O King.

REBEL: . . . who owns nothing.

CHORUS: Rise, O King.

REBEL: Desert menders, baptize me.

*With outstretched arms he lowers his
face against the ground. One of the
men pours dirt on his head and neck.*

Mealy earth, milk of my mother, warm on my neck, rich
rivulet, semidarkness, demand, direct . . .

He places his ear to the ground.

O! countries, pounding hooves, fat larvae crawling in the val-
ley of my ears . . . I am invested. Oh, oh, I am invested.

He straightens up.

Chargers of the night, take me away.

ACT 3

REBEL: Darkness of the pit I hail you.

JAILER, *to the audience:* Look at him, a caricature if there ever was one, his bearing unstable, his face overripe, his hands clammy, the hypocritical and sly leader of a nation of savages, the pathetic guide of a demonic race, a sly schemer lost among the frenzied . . .

REBEL: Attached like a pennant to the very top of the country, I'm not sobbing, I'm calling.

JAILER: We have mined out the echo, your words shall burn like excrement.

REBEL: I have managed to grow a tree of sulphur and lava amidst a defeated people.
The race made of dirt the race in the dirt discovered it had feet
let the Congo and Mississippi flow with gold
flow with blood
the race made of dirt, the race made of ashes is walking
the feet on the road explode into saltpeter bits.

JAILER: You will pay, prisoner of hunger, of loneliness, of despair.

REBEL: No. The landscape is poisoning me with the aconite of its alphabet. Blind, I intuit my eyes and the cloud is the head of the old nigger I saw thrashed to death on a public square, the low sky is stuffy, the wind rolls burdens and the sobs of sweating skin, the wind is contaminated with whips and tuns and the hanged populate the sky with

Aimé Césaire

male orchises and there are bulldogs their hair bloody
  and ears . . . ears . . . boats made of severed ears gliding
  over the sunset.
Leave me be, man, I am alone and the sea is a shackle around
  my convict ankle.

CHORUS: Pity, I ask for pity.

REBEL: Who said pity?
Who is trying to erase the black and fiery spectacle with this
  inappropriate word? Who is asking for mercy?
Do I ask for mercy for my blinded eyes?
Do I not endure my irreparable visions?
And I do not need a harpoon, and I do not need a cleav-
  ing axe.
No forgiveness.
Along with my heart I brought back the ancient flint, the old
  amadou deposited by Africa in the depths of my being.
I hate you. I hate all of you.
And my hatred will not die
as long as the obese sun rides the sorry nag of the Earth.
And now the living past is putting forth leaves
the past shreds like a banana leaf.
The cataclysm with its scalped head, its brain of cogwheels of
  larvae and of watches
at the mercy of fables
at the mercy of expiatory victims
is waiting
its eyes capsized by magnetic palavers.
Freedom, freedom,
I alone will risk bearing the light of this wounded head.

The messenger enters.

CHORUS: Ah, here comes the worthy messenger of this
  greedy race.
Their pallid complexion has been woven out of gold and
  silver.

And the Dogs Were Silent

Waiting for prey has hooked their bestial noses
a steel gleam nests in their frigid eyes
Ah, a race without velvet.

MESSENGER: Hail.

REBEL: O my limbs of smashed walls
you will not extinguish my fatigue and my cold
my smoking cry my intact cry of a trapped animal.

MESSENGER: I said, hail.

REBEL: Who calls me? I listen I don't listen.
In my head there's a river of mud of bleaks of murky green
    things, of dead birds, of yellow bellies,
of crisscrossed meowings squirting right out of the gag
my convulsed years painted in fire
turntables of swamps
In my ears there is
a firing squad in the caponiers of the morning.

NARRATOR: A warlike trumpet rang through the air: it was
    spitting dust and smoke.

NARRATOR: Monkeys were cavorting around the human-
    faced lion.

REBEL: I fear nothing my friends
today is a day of complicity.
There are days bitter to my lips and the wild mango that falls
    falls lugubriously and the flowers resemble women buried
    alive who respond more and more feebly, but today I am
    at peace—the filagos make signs to me and the sea smiles
    at me with all of its dimples and each manchineel dupli-
    cates itself and severs itself from the propitious olive.
Day of reckoning, I welcome you.

Pause.

Well! Here you are, worthy messenger of the master race.
    Their flared nostrils having sniffed out the nearby trea-

sure our masters have assigned you the task of revealing our little secrets . . . par for the course . . . no civet cat runs faster on the tracks of a gazelle.

Pause.

Swallow your message
I want to die here
alone
hey, don't pull a long face
I know your message . . .
my freedom, right?
but the colonialist the legitimate owner of the sugarcane the clairin the cocoa bean and coffee
will display his mug of a table of contents and requiescat in the four quarters of our weariness
and he will make our black women pregnant with mulatresses
peacefully as he likes
right?
and then again this . . .

Parodically.

. . . back to work, swine,
if you're not back pronto your very lives will be cursed . . .
anolis will suck at the balls of your feet . . . menfenils will   *
peck at your liver . . . tafia will make termites hatch in your throats . . . wasps will nest in your eyes . . . and when you die (from ugly fat and laziness), you'll be the lousy niggers condemned to plant sugarcane and to hoe on the moon where there are no breadfruit trees . . . All right, we understand . . . that we are to have the patience of termites, and for a gentle disposition that of crabs who scuttle to the side when given a kick in the snout—and for docility, that of the stars, I mean that of the ticks bursting under the heels of clouds.

Raving.

O leave me alone, leave me alone.
What do you want of me? Why are you dead set against me?

And the Dogs Were Silent

True, you do not know who I am. Look how elegant my arms are, look at the delicacy of my hands.

Hatefully.

So, scram, I mean come back tomorrow . . . that's it . . . you've understood . . . I was sure of it . . . all the same, one is better off alone . . .

and no hard feelings, eh . . . and I will utter the great black scream so forcefully that the world's foundations will be shaken.

The messenger backs off stage.

NARRATRESS: I say that this country is an ulcer.

NARRATOR: I say that this land burns.

NARRATRESS: Beware: a curse on whoever brushes his hand across the resin of this country.

NARRATOR: I say that this country is a monstrous devourer.

NARRATRESS: This country is cursed.
This country yawns, having spit up the hookworm Cuba, a mouth of empty clamoring.

NARRATOR: This country bites: mouth open over a throat of fire the convergence of fiery fangs on the rump of evil America.

NARRATRESS: At the edge of skittering tides I walk on the water of revolving springs and I perceive my sentry eyes very high above. Foolproof insomnia increases like a disobedience along the free days of the woman with the amphora, water bearer, water bearer, germ storm, kettle.

REBEL: With my hands I disentangle thoughts that are lianas without contracture, and I hail my total brotherhood.
Rivers thrust into my flesh their squirrel-monkey snouts
forests grow in the mangrove fruit of my muscles
the breakers of my blood sing in the keys.
I shut my eyes

Aimé Césaire

all my riches under my hands
all my swamps
all my volcanoes
my rivers hang from my neck like snakes and precious
    necklaces.

NARRATOR: He is standing in the roar of the river . . . from
    the golden bank a hundred warriors hurl a hundred as-
    segais at him . . . his chest is lunate with scars.

NARRATRESS: It is the day of reckoning.
The rebel is naked. In his left hand is a plaited straw shield . . .
he stops, he crawls . . . he kneels motionless on the ground . . .
    his torso is as inverted as a wall. His assegai is raised . . .

> *At that moment a cortege from medi-*
> *eval Africa pours out onto the stage:*
> *a magnificent reconstitution of an-*
> *cient Benin civilization.*

FIRST TEMPTER'S VOICE: My voice rustles with silken
    words
my voice breathes umbellate plumes
my seasonless voice between the basins scoops out a thousand
    harmonious dreams
my voice of eyelashes sharpens to perfection a thousand tri-
    umphant insects
my voice is a beautiful bird blazing with gold
with the silken veil of the sky with unconstrained desire
my humid voices roll rivulets of doves unfrightened across
    pebbles of jasper and ecbatane . . .   *

REBEL: Who is she, the hidden one who pierces me with
    gold and silver and besieges me with the perils of un-
    known caresses?

NARRATOR: I questioned the sacred dice. I say that there
    lives in you a regal being sleeping on a bed too narrow for
    him.

And the Dogs Were Silent

REBEL: I say that we've given a new swing to the bell of the
world by ringing three golden words . . .

FIRST TEMPTER'S VOICE: Ha, Ha, Ha, words, nothing
but words: is it money you want? titles? land? King . . .
that's it . . . you will be king . . . I swear you will be king.

REBEL: I pull out one foot
Oh I pull out the other foot
without insulting me with promises let me unstick myself
from the carrion and the mud . . .

SECOND TEMPTER'S VOICE: . . . a king, what an adven-
ture. And it's true, there's something in you that could
never submit, an anger, a desire, a sadness, an impa-
tience, finally a scorn, a violence . . . and behold, your
veins are carrying gold not mud, pride not servitude.
King, you were formerly a king.

REBEL: Nocturnal feast
the cloven houses dribble forth their abstract cup of fer-
de-lance
serpents and rose windows
cities burst like sheep of black vomit
the swollen river struts like a peacock
on the broken dike
windows open on forever
stop the torture cruise of Edens blocked by turbations   *
at the seashore a countryside of rum and contraband
unfolds the smooth fever of the days
by means of nested suns.

CHORUS: Bornu, Sokoto Benin and Dahomey, Sikasso
Sikasso
I sound the assembly: skies and breasts, mists and pearls, sow-
ings, gold keys.

REBEL: Martinique, Jamaica
all the mirages and all the mango birds
cannot make the gunshot the wasted blood the song of steel

fraternal abysses of Jericho roses
ring with dormant oblivion.

CHORUS: You will not escape your own law, which is the
law of domination.

REBEL: My law is that I should run on an unbroken chain
until the fiery joining that volatilizes me purifies me and
ignites me with my amalgamated gold prism.

CHORUS: A taste of ruins; a funereal kiss; the moon is on
the wane, the king is hiding.

REBEL: I will not be the drop of perfume in which the count-
less sacrifices of disarmed roses are summed up and
celebrated.

NARRATOR: You will perish.

NARRATRESS: Alas, you will perish.

REBEL: So, I will perish. But naked. Intact.
My hand in my own hand, my foot on the ground,
what is this dark crumbling into the sunset flanked by
drowned bodies and bow nets?
Murdered by circumlocution, caught in the net of its own pa-
renthesis, the world is sinking.
Naked like water
naked like the unicorn look of noon
like the scream and the bite
I clarify the low vapors
on this world that is without knowledge and without in-
gratitude
where thought is unequivocally a flower with a butterfly's heart
I want a naked world made of unstamped universe
a little Fouta girl gnaws at a bone shaped like a candelabra
and I am young, I am opulent with youth, of a childhood from
before doors and windows, of a childhood of libation and
holocausts eye after eye hour after hour. A lake of dry-
ness hangs from my cheek, but it is crying eyes over the
Judas trees bathed in crocuses and anemones.

And the Dogs Were Silent

I am naked
I am naked in the stones
I want to die.

NARRATRESS: Be patient, I'm looking, I have watched.
My polar head gulps down the glimmerings of cadavers, cracked helmets, inconsolable debris.

REBEL: I am not an octopus, I will not spit night and ink into the face of death.

NARRATRESS: A reckless girl breaks her shell of disaster, coyote marksmen awaken in a hut of happy absinthe.

REBEL: Come closer then tapering flames, bundles of shivers. Let the fire scent hurl its javelin at my head.

NARRATRESS: And all that remains now is a lost man, as tragic as the stump of a palm tree in a vapid riot and a field of thunder. His dusty eyes throw themselves onto the shadeless and waterless steppe
and he chews shade and water
a prayer that he will not sell . . .

REBEL: . . . my cobra prayer . . . my moray prayer in the forests of the sea
my cactus-milk prayer in the brushwood of the sky . . .

NARRATRESS: . . . I watched: the bridges are dynamited . . .
the stars have incised their scars of sand.

REBEL: Ha, Ha
we no longer see
ha, ha,
we are blind
blind by the grace of god and by fear
and you see nothing in the new grass?
nothing in the churning of the earth and the convulsive vegetal racket
nothing in the sea, right?
I see, I hear . . . I shall speak out . . .
oh new sucking at my blood by the vampire sun

oh assault on my rock by the corsair night—under their
   muzzles my dawn has burst out with a crash of noon and
   seagulls.
Bind me,
trample me. Murder me. Too late.
The flushed-forth hours are striking over the calms and an-
   chor lights
the sniffling hours are striking
and they lengthen at the stroking of my hands
the flames lengthen
I too am a flame
I am the hour
I hear what the wind says
that firebrand tongue in my bone-dry throat.

CHORUS, *acting as a crowd:* He is king . . . he lacks the title,
   but undoubtedly he is king . . .
a true Lamido . . . here are his guards . . . their silver helmets   *
   blazing in the sunset.

NARRATOR: The king is cold . . . the king shivers . . . the
   king is coughing.

NARRATRESS: Alas, alas, arachnoid Europe is moving her
   fingers and her phalanxes of ships . . . Alas, alas.

CROWD-CHORUS: My memories are delirious with incense
   and bells . . . the blue Niger . . . the golden Congo . . .
   the sandy Logone . . . a gallop of hartebeests . . . and the
   millet pounders in the cobalt evening.

NARRATOR: My memories troat the kidnapping . . . the car-
   can . . . the tracks in the forest . . .
the baracoon . . . the slave ship.

SEMICHORUS: They would brand us with red-hot irons . . .

REBEL: And we would be sold like beasts, and they would
   count our teeth . . . and they would probe our balls, and
   they would examine the shine or decline of our skin—
   they would grope us and weigh us and reweigh us and

And the Dogs Were Silent

would encircle our tamed animal necks with the collars of servitude and nicknames.

NARRATOR: The wind picked up,
the savannahs split crazily into a glory of plumes . . . I hear children's cries in the master's house . . .

REBEL: I hear children's cries in the blacks' shacks . . . and the tiny stony bellies bulging through their overgrown navels are swollen with hunger, with the black mush of earth and tears and snot and urine.

NARRATOR: In the name of all the disintegrated desires in the pond of your souls.

NARRATRESS: In the name of all the lazy dreams in your hearts I sing the matador's steel thrust.

NARRATOR: I sing the harpooner's salty thrust and the whale spouting for the last time.

CHORUS: A bird and her smile . . . a ship and her roots . . . the horizon and her locks of precious stones . . . a young woman with a grassy smile shreds the wine of days, the stone of nights, into slender larks . . .

REBEL: Enough,
I'm afraid, I'm alone
my forests are earless my rivers fleshless
unknown galleons roam the night.
Is it you, Columbus? Skipper of the slave ship? Is it you old pirate, old corsair?
The night increases in debris.
Columbus, Columbus,
Answer me, please answer me:
beautiful like the shadow womb of two pitons at noon
the archipelago
a turbulence of lying organs
a sacrifice of lamp glasses crossed on the mouths of tempests
virulent turmoil caught absurdly in the movement of pastures and scolopendras

it's me tonight cursing the entire forest gathered into rings of
    violent screams
Columbus, Columbus,

ECHO. FIRST VOICE, *ironically:* Glory to the restorer of
    the fatherland.

ECHO. SECOND VOICE, *ironically:* Glory and gratitude to
    the educator of the people.

ECHO. CHORISTERS, *bawling:* salvum fac gubernatorem!!

REBEL: Isles of the blessed
gardens of the queen
I set myself adrift in the night of spices of tornadoes and of
    holy icons
and the kelp grips with its tiny children's fingers my trumpet-
    ing future of jetsam.

CHORISTERS, *bawling:* salvum fac civitatis fundatorem!!

REBEL: A tower
there are cracks in the wall: I see a comet above
a forest full of wolves
and there they encircle—mitres on their heads—
a dish of poisonous mushrooms
then they attack it gluttonously.

CHORISTERS IN THE WINGS, *bawling louder:* salvum fac
    . . .

REBEL: Away with you
go
you rats I pity you
rats sensing the ship is rotten
go, go in peace
remove your painted carcasses
your pious carcasses.

CHORISTERS, *bawling:* salvum fac . . .

REBEL: A monkey, I am a monkey who by his grimaces
    gathers into a mob the ports of call, the puddles, the

powder mills of despair, suppressed starvation and ven-
geance, nuclear perils, unmentionable devotions
and it is you I interrogate
oh wind
calm contorted guano-painted face
desert wind erected with cactus and sphinx
calamitously
did you hear something?

NARRATOR, *sneering:* The fleet of fleets:
the armada of fate.

NARRATRESS: Oh, the rise of batardeaux:
an agony over the waters
a voice in the cistern
the rainy cheetah's gruff voice
in the cistern in the forest of the ocean.

REBEL: Here is my querencia.   *

NARRATRESS: . . . a throng of porpoises of conspiring frig-
ates an avant-garde of *vocero* singers and gravediggers   *
. . .

> *Priests of every order giving frantic*
> *blessings fill the stage.*

REBEL: Goddamn it,
get the hell out of here, you—goddamn it
do the executioners not test their axes on the block?
Do the birds of prey not violate the circles around their eyes?
Is it in order to see that the pyramids stand on tiptoes
tonight?

NARRATOR: The moment has come when in the boggy night
the noiseless trap begins to function.

NARRATRESS: The moment has come when with a heavy
hand a shadow projects itself on the assassinated wall.

NARRATOR: The moment has come when clean of insects
and parasites all words are beautiful and deadly.

NARRATRESS: The moment has come when murderous rain
   sharpens to the core each stone tooth in the field.

CHORUS: Man, all of today's words are for you.
Man, all the words of man are staring at you.

REBEL: And I want to scream and I shall be heard at the end
   of the world (*he screams*)
my son, my son.

NARRATOR: The son is arriving.

REBEL, *pretending to rock a child:* Three black children are
   playing in my eye
nudged by dogs
and the open galaxies in my hand thunderstrike the landscape
of moanings
of leprosies
of elephantiasis
of dismissed charges of denials of justice of lynching of slow
   death
pickaninnies
and your untamed laughter
larval laughter
eggy laughter
your laughter a flaw in their steel
your laughter a crack in the wall
your laughter a heresy in their dogmas
your laughter that tattoos coins behind their backs
your incurable laughter
your laughter a vertigo into which mesmerized cities will sink
your laughter a time bomb under their masters' feet
toucan
disastrous wind
sprinkled with strong liquors
pickaninnies gnawed by the sun
beware of the malevolent stain of the sun
of the sun cancer inching toward your heart
until—laughter of

And the Dogs Were Silent

your bare feet—the world
falls
the great crazy flight of a struck hen.

He laughs frenetically.

NARRATRESS: The son is arriving.

NARRATOR: The son is arriving.

CHORUS: Behold, the son is arriving.

REBEL: That's good; I ask for a torch and my son arrives.

NARRATRESS: Behold, the son is arriving.

REBEL: A treasure, but it is I who demand the return of my
    stolen treasure,
London, Paris, New York, Amsterdam
I see them all gathered around me like stars, like triumphal
    moons
and with my poor eyes, my rotten breath, my blindman fin-
    gers groping for the lock,
I want to calculate
ah, to calculate under their calm and their dignity and their
    equilibrium and their movement and their noise and their
    harmony and their measure,
what it took of my nervous energy
of my panic
of my screams of an eternal bum—how many thimblefuls of
    sweat from my sweating face—to achieve this, my son!

> *Music as hot as possible; the piano
> sneers; flights and zigzags from the
> clarinet, overtaken from time to time
> with a great slap on the back by the
> jovial laughter of the trombone.*
>
> *The prison is surrounded by a vocif-
> erous mob carrying torches, shouting
> insults. Behind bars, the Rebel.*

Aimé Césaire

AN ORATOR, *pointing at the Rebel:* Comrades, the point is that that man is a public enemy and a bothersome bastard. As if we did not have enough trouble as it is? Sure, we were not happy. But Comrades, are we happy now that we have to deal with the masters' war and revenge? So I say he betrayed us.

REBEL: Pit of scorpions.

CROWD-CHORUS: To death with him.

REBEL: Cowards in your voices I hear the chafing of the harness.

CROWD-CHORUS: To death, to death with him.

REBEL: In your jackal voices a nostalgia for muzzles.

CROWD-CHORUS: Death, death . . .

REBEL: Ah, I pity you wasted souls: all the agedness of the world on your cannibalistic youth that knows no hope nor despair . . .

CROWD-CHORUS: Kill him, kill him. To death with him!

REBEL: May hell crash on your heads! To my aid, O death, my icy-handed militiaman.

CROWD-CHORUS: Long live peace.

REBEL: Long live vengeance;
the mountains will shake like a tooth in the forceps
the stars will break their foreheads of gravid women against the earth . . .

CROWD-CHORUS: Listen to him, listen to him . . .

REBEL: . . . halted the suns will turn the light into catastrophic coconut trees . . .

CHORUS: Curse him, curse him.

REBEL: Ah, you will not leave until you've felt my words tear into your imbecilic souls

for know that I stalk you as my prey . . .
and I watch you and strip you naked of your lies and of your
    cowardliness
vain flunkies puny hypocrites obeisant
slaves and sons of slaves
and you no longer have the strength to protest, to be ashamed
    of your moaning,
condemned to a tête-à-tête with stinking stupidity, without
    anything to keep your blood warm other than watching
your half-jigger of Antillean rum shimmer . . .
Sluttish souls.

CROWD-CHORUS: Bravo, bravo!

REBEL: My friends
I dreamt of light, of golden banners, of enpurpled sleeps of
    besparkled
awakenings and of lynx pelts.

CROWD-CHORUS: Bravo, death to the tyrants!

REBEL: And indeed, from the gasping catacombs of the end
    and the beginning
death is rushing toward them like a torrent of maddened
    horses, like a swarm of mosquitoes . . .

JAILER: Silence.

REBEL: All right, worthy citizens, it's true that I'm a bother . . .
    and that you would like to silence me . . . frighten me,
    frighten me utterly, I am a great coward you know: I have
    shuddered from all terrors since the primordial terror.

JAILER: The rogue!

REBEL: Frighten me, frighten me good I tell you. And you
    know just how to do it: tighten a rope around my fore-
    head, hang me by the armpits, heat up my soles with a
    red-hot shovel.

JAILER: Shut up for god's sake.

REBEL: Run a red-hot padlock through my mouth!

Aimé Césaire

JAILER'S WIFE: He's tempting me!

REBEL: Brand my shoulder with a fleur-de-lis, a prison bolt, or with just a ligature of your initials, Jean or Pierre or Jeanne or Louise or Geneviève ... yes ... or with a flag ... or with a cannon ... or a cross ... or a clover ...

JAILER: All the devils in hell are stirring the fire in his swinish black hide.

REBEL: ... or else with your intertwined monograms or with a Latin formula ...

JAILER: Enough.

REBEL: They feign scruples. Don't be embarrassed. I was absent at the baptism of Christ!

JAILER: Anyone can see that!

REBEL: And I accuse myself of having laughed at Noah, my naked father my drunken father
and I accuse myself of having wallowed from love in the opaque night, in the heavy night.

JAILER'S WIFE: Smack him, smack him, it'll be good for his swinish hide!

REBEL: Who are you, woman?
I've known women; breasts surprised in the pasture ...

JAILER'S WIFE: Hey, the lout's insulting me: the bastard, he's insulting me, you hear?

JAILER: Insolent, disgusting, libidinous ape!

> *He strikes him; the wife also
> strikes him.*

CHORUS: Let his blood flow.

SEMICHORUS: Let it flow.

CHORUS: I will not moan about it.

And the Dogs Were Silent

SEMICHORUS: O honey itself is not as sweet as this blood is rich and salty.

REBEL: The king . . . repeat: the king!
all the violence of the dead world
beaten with rods, given over to beasts
dragged in his shirt a rope around his neck
doused with gasoline
and I awaited the hour of the auto-da-fé in my sanbenito
and trampled, betrayed, sold, I drank urine
and I ate excrement
and I acquired the power to speak
louder than rivers
more forcefully than disasters

JAILER: Eh, is this coon making fools of us . . . for sure he's playing the fool.
harder, still harder . . .

He strikes.

REBEL: Hit him . . . hit him, overseer . . . beat him until he bleeds . . . from the furrows an unmoaning race was born . . . beat him until you give out.

JAILER'S WIFE: A rock; what a rock. He's a rock I tell you . . . a funny race those niggers . . . do you think our blows hurt him? In any case they don't show (*she strikes*). Oh oh, some blood.

JAILER: He's trying to scare us, let's take off . . .

JAILER'S WIFE: Why he's plumb out of his mind . . . I could die laughing. . . . Hey, red blood on black skin *is weird.*

REBEL, *jolted:* Severed hands . . . spurting brain . . . soft carrion
why stay on under a rain of venomous scorpions?
Anteaters wandering in time are licking aquamarine ants from village pavements. In the joints between equinoxes opossums are looking for

Aimé Césaire

a russet tree a silver tree
in the muddy putty of fatalities and the hide-and-seek of glow-
    worms a volition is convulsing.

He collapses moaning.

NARRATRESS: What a night; what a wind; it's as if the wind
    and the night had had a furious struggle: great masses of
    darkness are collapsing with the entire sky panel and the
    cavalry of the wind rushes into flight whipped by a hun-
    dred thousand burnooses.

*The wind carries snatches of
spirituals.*

REBEL: Everything fades, everything crumbles
all that I care for now are my recollected skies
all that I have left is a stairway to descend step by step
all that I have left is the little rose of a stolen ember
a scent of naked women
a country of fabulous explosions
an icecap's peal of laughter
a necklace of desperate pearls
an obsolete calendar
the taste, the vertigo, the luxury of exhilarating sacrilege.
Kings magi
their eyes protected by three rows of honeycombed eyelids
salt of grey noons
distilling thorn by thorn a meager path
a lost trail
a stratum of regrets and expectations
ghosts caught in the crazed circles of black-blooded rocks
I'm thirsty
oh, how thirsty I am
in quest of peace and of verdant light
I plunged the entire pearly season
into a sewer
blind to everything
burning.

And the Dogs Were Silent

NARRATRESS: Curses crushed under stones throb across the path with the heavy eyes of toads; a great demented noise shakes the island by its sky, tragic bones roll against nature, a badly drained and diseased night surrounds the world.

CHORUS: I remember morning on the islands
morning kneading almond and glass
thrushes laughing in the pod tree
and the cane juice did not smell bad
no
not in the succulent morning!

REBEL: I'm searching for the traces of my power as a bush-man would look for the lost tracks of a great herd and I sink to my knees in the tall grass of the blood.
Pitiful gods, good-natured faces, long dangling arms, expelled from a paradise of rum, ashy palms haunted by bats and sleepwalking packs!
Rise, fumes, light up the disaster . . .
I bled in secret corridors, on the churned-open battlegrounds
And
I advance, a tarnished fly a huge malicorne and voracious   *
   insect
attracted by the delights of my own saw-toothed skeleton,
legacy of my assassinated body violent across the bars of the sun.

NARRATOR: Flayed, scattered
on the grounds in the thickets
gutted poem.

NARRATRESS: The island bleeds.

NARRATOR: The island bleeds.

NARRATRESS: Cul-de-sac of misery, of solitude, of stinking weeds.

REBEL: The caiman the torches the flags
and the Amazon erect with heveas

Aimé Césaire

and moons floated down like winged seeds through the tepid
    compost of the sky
my soul is swimming at the very heart of the maelstrom
where strange monograms germinate
a drowned man's phallus, a tibia, a sternum . . .

Here great hallucinatory shadows
and grim nightmarish realities fill the
prison.

FIRST SUBTERRANEAN VOICE: O King.

SECOND SUBTERRANEAN VOICE: Rise, O King.

FIRST WHISPERING: Horses of the night.

SECOND WHISPERING: Take him away, take him away.

REBEL: Do they expect to have me as if I was a wild boar
    and her young?
To extirpate me like a root without descendants? Words,
between high salt banks, between gorges, you wind your way,
    I hail you, dragging up your booty of things patiently
    scraped from the great depths, you wind your way.
You, mouth, be poised,
muted name of the enormous wound!

A pause.

Mares of fire, will I still know how to bristle up your manes in
    the hollow of my breath?
O! my pitiful heroes.
Those who come from Dahomey, having brought along a
treasure, *only* their lips shut on some elemental formulas
a knowledge of plants the harshness of dying
tall lords of the drum
Those from a spasmatic Congo
(our life—Mayumbe, how you tore at its deaf Fortune with
    your Congolese fangs!)
Those who in order to come had crossed high forests, vast
    deserts, above all an endless sea,

And the Dogs Were Silent

Those who had been bitten by the harmattan and battered by
     trade winds
and then by shame and pain and rage
and spittle more abundant even than the sea!
And you, knights of the hoe,
princesses of the vetiver
paladins of the cutlass
(Ibos, our Ibibio life, how you wrapped around our necks
     your maze of marshes, of rivers, of mangrove swamps)
Rubbish, adventure of my thirst, oblivion three-quarters drunk!
Oh the warriors, the slaves, the maroons, the sorcerers, my
     blood, a treasure rescued from thorns, rounded image,
     loyal blood,
and you, comrades,
drain-makers, cutters, binders, pirogue paddlers,
(our life—a raped, forsaken wasteland, how you reduced it,
     Fortune,
to grey weeds dry weeds sad humiliated weeds)
Oh! so many stranded paths,
so many crumbled waters,
so many collapsed lands,
so many evasive banks,
and here I stand suddenly null mouth embittered alone truly
     yourself
here I stand in the middle of the road
my feet muddy, I stop, it is hot
I bandage my toes and suddenly before resuming the journey
I raise my face toward the core of the sky. Clear hour watched
     over by sphinxes
this is the place!
As for me, Crossroad, if you should weigh us
on your dust scales, I will be no less heavy than the filtered
water of my voice
for what opens the way
is equally the scream sprung from the muddy hollow of the
     faithful attentive lode.
Let it be known: if one could choose,

Aimé Césaire

Tenebrous-faithful-Memory-and Coulter-of-the-future
I would erect this name in the live hollow of the current.

Pause.

Let's say
three women
the first pierced us with her sword
the red one dressed us in the inheritance of her blood
the third one
I resurrected her voice left half dead by the flint
I wetted her lips with my saliva and I sang
the song: "Sweet light guide us."

Pause.

Therefore I welcome you, obstacle!
through which multiple and difficult I discover myself
and you, rhythm, perpetual influx, perpetual reflux,
in my black ungrateful stone the daba of blood
and my answer . . .

Pause.

. . . and I rise, and I hold firm
amidst all these torrents carriers
of branches, of mud and snakes.
It is true, I have in my ear the grey wind of beratings,
but what do I care about beratings,
I know the hour, my lands, my sowings.
At the height of my human chest, in the unplowed land of the
    sun
I still say who grows the beautiful millet of hope!
Sure and winged seed, I am ready!
settled clod, I'm ready, pent-up flood, I'm ready!

FIRST CELESTIAL VOICE: Sunflowers of shadow, incline
    your compass faces toward the blackest of midnights . . .

SECOND CELESTIAL VOICE: Let tortures be invented for
    me, let the oliphant sound, a strand of rope
strand of rope . . .

And the Dogs Were Silent

CHORUS, *subterraneously:* Here is my hand, here is my hand
my cool hand, my hand of a jet of water of blood
my hand of kelp and of iodine
my hand of light and of vengeance . . .

REBEL: You gods down there, benevolent gods
I'm carrying off in my broken-down mug
the buzzing of a living flesh
here I am . . .

Pause.

. . . a rumble of chains of carcans rises from the sea . . .
a gurgling of the drowned from the green belly of the sea . . . a
    crackling
of fire the cracking of a whip, cries of the murdered . . .
. . . the sea is burning
or it's the packing of my blood that is burning . . .
oh the scream . . . always this scream bursting from the
    mornes . . . and the rutting of drums and in vain the
    wind swelling the tender odor of the moldy ravine
of breadfruit trees, of sugar mills, of bagasse harassed by
    gnats . . .
Earth my mother I understood your cloak-and-dagger language
my brothers the maroons the bits in their teeth
my brothers their feet sticking out of the pen and in the
    torrent
my sister the shooting star, my brother the crushed glass
my brother the bloody kiss of the severed head in the sil-
    ver dish
and my sister epizooty and my sister epilepsy
my friend the kite
my friend the conflagration
each drop of my blood explodes in the piping of my veins
and my brother the volcano with his pistol paunch
and my brother the precipice without a balisier parapet
and my mother, madness with her herbs of smoke and heresy
her feet of crusade and walking stick

Aimé Césaire

her hands of hibernation and of never
and of jujubes and of perturbation and of a bayoneted sun.

> *The Rebel starts to walk, to crawl,
> to run through imaginary thickets,
> naked warriors leap about, a remote
> tom-tom is heard.*

NARRATRESS: Oh the dance of nameless stars . . . the sav-
annahs stir . . . rain steams . . . unknown trees fall pal-
mate with thunder.

NARRATOR: What is she saying? What is she saying?

> *At that moment the Rebel straight-
> ens up.*

REBEL: Caterpillars crawl toward the inns of cotton night-
caps . . . The vat of the earth is extinguished . . . all
right . . . but the sky is eating betel nuts . . . ha, ha, the
sky is sucking daggers . . . King of Malaysia and of the
fever swarming with insects, chew well your kriss and
your betel nut . . . My son, my son, a ball is rotting be-
tween your white smiles . . . ay, I'm walking on star
spines. I'm walking . . . I'm taking charge . . . I'm em-
bracing . . .

> *The Rebel collapses, his arms out-
> stretched, his face against the ground;
> at that moment a frenetic burst of
> tom-toms blocks out the voices.*

REBEL: Leaning on the parapet of fire
the screams of clouds were not enough for me
Bark tom-toms
Bark dogs guardians of the lofty portal
dogs of nothingness
bark at the end of your rope
bark snake heart
bark scandal of the sweat room and of the grigri
bark fury of lymphs

And the Dogs Were Silent

council of ancient terrors
bark
demasted wrecks
even to the resignation of centuries and stars.

NARRATOR: Dead, he is dead!

NARRATRESS: Dead in a copse of perfumed clerodendrons.

NARRATOR: Dead right in the middle of growing sisal.

NARRATRESS: Dead right in the middle of the calabash pulp.

NARRATOR: Dead right in the middle of a volley of torches, in the middle of a fecundation of vanilla plants . . .

NARRATRESS: Secrets choked back by a twist of the gullet are ascending to the steeple of the blood. Possessed women raise their soapy hands in the four quarters of the red-hearted marsh; new thirsts flow forth, moons broken on the same loaf of water, a stone on a forehead.

NARRATOR: Unlanguishing kohl, the blasé atmosphere of an open door is miraculous, a precious annatto sneer. A compass is dying of convulsions on a sandy moor, a bowl of milk at the end of the world.

NARRATRESS: In the forest the murderesses flow with fountain laughter, and rivers without signals plot the fleshy adventures of virulent voyages.
Let the nomadic blood flirting with death and genesis
waste the deadly laughter of cavernous mummies at the bottom
of pitted stones and the night of centuries!

NARRATOR: Watchtowers, crumble!

NARRATRESS: Revenge towers, crumble lower than words!

NARRATOR: Parasitic plants, poisonous plants, burning plants, cannibal plants, incendiary plants, true plants, trickle forth your unforeseen curves in fat drops.

NARRATRESS: Light decomposed in each avaricious splendor,

Aimé Césaire

cargo of golden fish, bedraggled fruit,
river on my thunderstruck lips.

NARRATOR: Orgy, orgy, divine water, star of luxurious
    flesh, vertigo
islands cool rings on the ears of plunging sirens
islands coins fallen from the star-filled pouch.

CHORUS: The swarming of larvae, worthless talismans
islands
silent islands
truncated islands . . .

NARRATOR: I come to you.

NARRATRESS: Islands, I am one of you!

> *Narrator and Narratress go weak in*
> *the knees before collapsing; the*
> *chorus exits backwards.*

> *Vision of the blue Caribbean*
> *spangled with gold and silver islands*
> *in the scintillation of the dawn.*

Translators' Notes

When we were working on our *Aimé Césaire: The Collected Poetry* (Berkeley and Los Angeles: University of California Press, 1983), we discovered that a number of runover lines in volume 1 of Césaire's *Oeuvres complètes* had been set as if they were two or more lines. Césaire asked us to make corrections in both the English and the French texts. In the present texts, we ran into the same problem not only in volume 2 of the *Oeuvres complètes,* but also in the Seuil edition of *moi, laminaire* . . . Based on our previous experience, and Césaire's encouragement to make corrections, we have again treated runovers as single lines.

In many cases, we have respected the unconventional and excessively arbitrary punctuation and capitalizations. Occasionally, we have added dashes, commas, or periods, as appropriate, for clarity.

We extend our gratitude to the Guadeloupean novelist Maryse Condé, who made a number of helpful suggestions concerning the meaning of obscure words.

P. 8: *poto-poto:* mud of a mangrove swamp. According to Condé, it is also a district of Brazzaville on the Congo River, and the phrase "l'art poto-poto" suggests "popular art."

P. 8: *piton:* "fewer in number than mornes [see following note] pitons are much more fantastic in form;—volcanic cones, or volcanic upheavals of splintered strata almost at right angles,—sometimes sharp of line as spires and mostly too steep for habitation. They are occasionally mammiform." (Lafcadio Hearn, *Two Years in the French West Indies* [New York: Harpers, 1890], p. 255).

P. 14: *morne:* "used throughout the French West Indian colonies to designate certain altitudes of volcanic origin, the word is justly applied to the majority of Martinique hills, and unjustly sometimes even to its mightiest elevation,— called . . . Montagne Pelée. . . . Mornes usually have . . . beautiful and curious forms . . . : they are most often pyramidal or conoid up to a certain height; but have summits either rounded or truncated; their sides, green with the richest vegetation, rise from valley-levels and coast-lines with remarkable abruptness." (Hearn, *Two Years,* pp. 254–55). In Césaire's youth, mornes were often the hillocks on the outskirts of towns on which slum areas were located.

P. 15: *Christophoric:* Césaire may be referring to Christophorus, a Roman prince of the eighth century who helped overthrow Pope Constantine and rallied the Franks. He was caught in a battle and had his eyes gouged out. It seemed to us that blindness was the idea, rather than prophetic leadership.

P. 23: *the shipwrecker's cow:* according to Professor Robert Ritchie of the department of history at the University of California at San Diego, there are two possible meanings here: in the seventeenth and eighteenth centuries, the Spanish crown populated many islands with cattle so as to provide sustenance for people who might land there or be shipwrecked. On the other hand, it could refer to the cow that buccaneers (also traditionally known as "cow killers") appropriated and killed for their own sustenance. Given the negative context in which the phrase appears, and the fact that *naufrageur* is usually an agent, we consider the second meaning as more likely.

P. 27: *clairin:* a sort of rum, or raw white alcohol, made from cane juice.

And the Dogs Were Silent

P. 28: *bombaïa:* a Haitian rallying cry associated with Boukman's voudou ceremonies at Bois Cayman on the eve of the 1791 revolts. Boukman, a black Haitian slave, became the leader of a number of ferocious revolts at this time at Noé, Clément, Flaville, Callifet, and Le Normand.

P. 29: *bayahonde:* a small shrub used in making fences.

P. 37: *fonio:* a cereal (*Digitaria exilis*) from West Africa.

P. 37: *shabeen:* from *chabin(e),* the French name for a kind of sheep crossbred from a ewe and a billygoat. Socially, in the West Indies, it refers to a mixed-race offspring. *Shabeen* is the term used in some English-speaking islands.

P. 39: *a good one:* based in French on "une pièce d'Inde," that is, "a thing from India," by which the slave traders described the handsomest and strongest slaves.

P. 41: *coui:* a half-calabash, used in making guitars, as well as drinking and eating vessels.

P. 46: *menfenil: Falco sparverius caribaearum,* the Caribbean sparrow hawk, also known as the *malfini.*

P. 48: *ecbatane:* according to the Bible, Ecbatana (today known as Hamadan) was the capital of ancient Media, where, following Cyrus's edict, Darius had a huge temple built to please the Jews. The temple was legendary for its numerous multicolored towers and for the endless treasures it contained. Césaire seems to have made an adjective of this proper name, evocative of multicolored magnificence.

P. 49: *turbation:* a medieval French word meaning "trouble," "confusion," "obstacle."

P. 52: *Lamido:* a famous Wolof warrior.

P. 55: *querencia:* Spanish, meaning "homing instinct," or "affection."

P. 55: *vocero:* Corsican funeral chant.

Aimé Césaire

P. 63: *malicorne:* in view of the adjectival use of this word, we feel that Césaire coined an adjective on *corne* (insect horns or antennae) and *mali* (evil), i.e., "an evil-horned insect."

P. 66: *daba:* a short-handled African hoe.

moi, laminaire . . .

i, laminaria . . .

moi, laminaire . . .

i, laminaria . . .

Le non-temps impose au temps la tyrannie de sa spatialité: dans toute vie il y a un nord et un sud, et l'orient et l'occident. Au plus extrême, ou, pour le moins, au carrefour, c'est au fil des saisons survolées, l'inégale lutte de la vie et de la mort, de la ferveur et de la lucidité, fût-ce celle du désespoir et de la retombée, la force aussi toujours de regarder demain. Ainsi va toute vie. Ainsi va ce livre, entre soleil et ombre, entre montagne et mangrove, entre chien et loup, claudiquant et binaire. Le temps aussi de régler leur compte à quelques fantasmes et à quelques fantômes.

Nontime imposes the tyranny of its spaciality on time: in any life there is a north and a south, and the east and the west. At the limit, or, any rate, at the crossroad, as one's eyes fly over the seasons, there is the unequal struggle of life and death, of fervor and lucidity, even if it is one of despair and collapse, the strength as well to face tomorrow. Such is life. Such is this book, between sun and shadow, between mountain and man-grove swamp, between dawn and dusk, lame and divided. Time also to settle one's account with a few phantoms and a few ghosts.

client et loup

calendrier lagunaire

j'habite une blessure sacrée
j'habite des ancêtres imaginaires
j'habite un vouloir obscur
j'habite un long silence
j'habite une soif irrémédiable
j'habite un voyage de mille ans
j'habite une guerre de trois cents ans
j'habite un culte désaffecté   *bulbe/tulip*
entre bulbe et caïeu j'habite l'espace inexploité
j'habite du basalte non une coulée
mais de la lave le mascaret
qui remonte la valleuse à toute allure
et brûle toutes les mosquées
je m'accommode de mon mieux de cet avatar
d'une version du paradis absurdement ratée
        —c'est bien pire qu'un enfer—
j'habite de temps en temps une de mes plaies
chaque minute je change d'appartement
et toute paix m'effraie

        tourbillon de feu
        ascidie comme nulle autre pour poussières
        de mondes égarés
        ayant craché volcan mes entrailles d'eau vive
        je reste avec mes pains de mots et mes minerais
        secrets   *peines*

---

8 2

I

lagoonal calendar

i inhabit a sacred wound
i inhabit imaginary ancestors
i inhabit an obscure will
i inhabit a long silence
i inhabit an irremediable thirst
i inhabit a one-thousand-year journey
i inhabit a three-hundred-year war
i inhabit an abandoned cult
between bulb and bulbil i inhabit the unexploited space
i inhabit not a vein of the basalt
but the rising tide of lava
which runs back up the gulch at full speed
to burn all the mosques
I make the most of this avatar
of an absurdly botched version of paradise
    —it is much worse than a hell—
i inhabit from time to time one of my wounds
each minute i change apartments
and any peace frightens me

    whirling fire
    ascidium like none other for the dust
    of strayed worlds
    having spat out my fresh-water entrails
    a volcano i remain with my loaves of words and
    my secret minerals

8 3

j'habite donc une vaste pensée
mais le plus souvent je préfère me confiner
dans la plus petite de mes idées
ou bien j'habite une formule magique
les seuls premiers mots
tout le reste étant oublié
j'habite l'embâcle
j'habite la débâcle
j'habite le pan d'un grand désastre
j'habite le plus souvent le pis le plus sec
du piton le plus efflanqué—la louve de ces nuages—
j'habite l'auréole des cactacées
j'habite un troupeau de chèvres tirant sur la tétine
de l'arganier le plus désolé
à vrai dire je ne sais plus mon adresse exacte
bathyale ou abyssale
j'habite le trou des poulpes
je me bats avec un poulpe pour un trou de poulpe

    frère n'insistez pas
    vrac de varech
    m'accrochant en cuscute
        ou me déployant en porana
    c'est tout un
        et que le flot roule
        et que ventouse le soleil
        et que flagelle le vent
    ronde bosse de mon néant

la pression atmosphérique ou plutôt l'historique
agrandit démesurément mes maux
même si elle rend somptueux certains de mes mots

i inhabit thus a vast thought
but in most cases i prefer to confine myself
to the smallest of my ideas
or else i inhabit a magical formula
only its opening words
the rest being forgotten
i inhabit the ice block
i inhabit the debacle
i inhabit the face of a great disaster
i inhabit in most cases the driest udder
of the skinniest peak—the she-wolf of these clouds—
i inhabit the halo of the Cactaceae
i inhabit a herd of goats pulling on the tit
of the most desolate argan tree
to tell you the truth i no longer know my correct address
bathyal or abyssal ~~fauna~~
i inhabit the octopuses' hole
i fight with an octopus over an octopus hole

deep
sea

    brother lay off
    wrack rubbish
    I hook on like devil's guts
        or uncoil poranalike   *
  it's all the same thing
      which the wave rolls
      which the sun cups
      which the wind flogs
  sculpture in the round of my nothingness

the atmospheric or rather historic pressure
even if it makes certain words of mine sumptuous
immeasurably increases my plight

la bonne nouvelle m'aura été portée à travers la cohue
   d'astres jaunes et rouges en fleurs pour la première fois par
   une volée de pouliches ivres

elles me disent que les phasmes se sont convertis en feuillage
   et acceptent de se constituer en forêts autonomes
qu'une fumée blanche monte du concile des quiscales pour
   annoncer que dans les zones les plus sombres du ciel des
   lucarnes se sont allumées

que le courant a été établi depuis le surfin du soleil jusqu'à la
   collerette des salamandres montant la garde aux tunnels
que la rouille est tombée en grêle libérant tout un imprévu de
   papillons

que les lamantins couverts de pierreries remontent les berges
que toute la cérémonie enfin a été ponctuée par le tir
   solennel des volcans installant de plein droit des lacs dans
   leur cratère
      poussants mon fol élan
      feuillants ma juste demeure
      racines ma survie
      une goutte de sang monte du fond
      seule incline le paysage
      et au faîte du monde
      fascine
         une mémoire irréductible

annonciades

the good news will have been brought to me through the
    throng of yellow and red stars in bloom for the first time
    by a flight of drunken fillies

they are telling me that the stick insects have turned into
    foliage and that they accept taking on the status of an
    autonomous forest
that a white smoke rises from the grackle council
    announcing that in the darkest zones of the sky lucarnes
    have lit up

that the current has been turned on from superfine sun to the
    collaret of salamanders keeping watch at the tunnels
that the rust fell like hail freeing a whole unforeseen of
    butterflies

that manatees covered with precious stones are climbing up
    the banks
that the whole ceremony in short was punctuated by the
    solemn shots of volcanoes installing on their own
    authority lakes in their craters
        growings my crazy ardor
        leafings my just dwelling
        roots my survival
        a drop of blood rises from the depths
        by itself tilts the landscape
        and at the crest of the world
        captivates
            an irreducible memory

3

la colline d'un geste mou saupoudrait
les confins des mangroves amères.
Aussitôt l'enlisement: je l'entendais claquer
du bec et reposer plus silencieusement
dans le scandale de ses mandibules.
Une complicité installait sa bave dans un remords
de sangsues et de racines.
On a tôt fait de médire des dragons: de temps en temps
l'un d'eux sort de la gadoue,
secouant ses ailes arrosant les entours et le temps
de disperser barques et hourques se retire
au large dans un songe de moussons.
Si de moi-même insu je marche suffocant d'enfances
qu'il soit clair pour tous que calculant les épactes
j'ai toujours refusé le pacte de ce calendrier lagunaire

3

with a limp gesture the hill sprinkled dust over
the borders of bitter mangrove swamps.
Instantly the quicksanding: i could hear it clacking
its beak and settling more silently
into the scandal of its mandibles.
A complicity installed its slime in the renewed bite
of leeches and of roots.
It is too easy to speak ill of dragons: from time to time
one emerges from the muck,
shaking its wings sprinkling its surroundings and hardly
has it scattered boats and hookers than it retreats
to open sea in a dream of monsoons.
If unbeknownst to myself i walk choking on childhoods
let it be clear to all that calculating the epacts
i've always rejected the pact of this lagoonal calendar

4

Léon G. Damas

feu sombre toujours . . .

(in memoriam)

des promesses qui éclatent en petites fusées
de pollens fous
des fruits déchirés
       ivres de leur propre déhiscence
la fureur de donner vie à un écroulement de paysages
(les aperçus devenant l'espace d'un instant
l'espace entier et toute la mémoire reconquise)
une donne de trésors moins abyssaux
que révélés (et dévoilés tellement amicaux)

et puis ces détonations de bambous annonçant sans répit
une nouvelle dont on ne saisit rien sur le coup
sinon le coup au cœur que je ne connais que trop

soleils
oiseaux d'enfance déserteurs de son hoquet
je vois les négritudes obstinées
les fidélités fraternelles
la nostalgie fertile
la réhabilitation de délires très anciens
je vois toutes les étoiles de jadis qui renaissent et sautent de
    leur site ruiniforme
je vois toute une nuit de ragtime et de blues
traversée d'un pêle-mêle de rires
et de sanglots d'enfants abandonnés

Léon G. Damas
somber fire always . . .

(in memoriam)

promises that burst into tiny missiles
of crazed pollen
torn fruit
        intoxicated with their own dehiscence
the passion to inject life into a collapse of landscapes
(insights turning into temporary space
the entire space and the whole memory reconquered)
a dealing out of treasures less abyssal ~faux~
than revealed (and once uncovered so friendly)

and then these detonations of bamboos relentlessly
    announcing
a bit of news that at first does not strike you at all
except in the heart in a way i know too well

suns
birds of childhood deserters from its hiccup
i see the stubborn negritudes
the fraternal fidelities
the fertile nostalgia
the rehabilitation of most ancient ravings
i see all the stars of yesteryear reborn and springing from
    their ruiniform sites
i see a whole night of ragtime and blues
pierced through by pell-mell laughter
and the sobs of abandoned waifs

et toi

qu'est-ce que tu peux bien faire là
noctambule à n'y pas croire de cette nuit vraie
salutaire ricanement forcené des confins
à l'horizon de mon salut

frère
              feu sombre toujours

and you

what on earth are you doing there
unbelievable sleepwalker of that true night
salubrious frenzied sneering of borders
on the horizon of my salute

brother
        somber fire always

5

les chercheurs de silex
les testeurs d'obsidienne
ceux qui suivent jusqu'à l'opalescence
l'invasion de l'opacité
les créateurs d'espace

allons les ravisseurs du Mot
les détrousseurs de la Parole
il y avait belle lurette qu'on leur avait signifié leur congé
de la manière la plus infamante.

testing . . .

the flint hunters
the obsidian assayers
those who follow the invasion of opacity
until it opalesces
the creators of space

oh, come on! the abductors of the Word
the highwaymen of Speech
were given notice ages ago
and most ignominiously.

par tous mots
guerrier-silex

le désordre s'organise évalueur des collines
sous la surveillance d'arbres à hauts talons
implacables pour tout mufle privé de la rigueur
des buffles

ça

le ça déglutit rumine digère
je sais la merde (et sa quadrature)
mais merde

que zèle aux ailes nourrisse le charognard bec
la pouture sans scrupules
tant le cœur nous défaut
faux le rêve si péremptoire la ronde
de ce côté du moins s'exsude
tout le soleil emmagasiné à l'envers
du désastre

car
    œil intact de la tempête

aurore
    ozone
        zone orogène

flint warrior
through all words

disorder organizes itself into an appraiser of hills
under the surveillance of high-heeled trees
merciless toward any muzzle
less rigorous than a buffalo's

it

the id swallows ruminates digests
i know shit (and its quadrature)
but shit

on zealous wings let the griffin vulture beak feed
the nonscrupulous stall-fattening
i have no heart for it
false the dream however peremptory the rounds
on this side at least
all the sun stored on the wrong side of disaster
exudes

for
[intact eye of the storm]

aurora
      ozone
            orogenic zone

par quelques-uns des mots obsédant une torpeur
et l'accueil et l'éveil de chacun de nos maux *mots*
je t'énonce
      FANON
tu rayes le fer
tu rayes le barreau des prisons
tu rayes le regard des bourreaux
guerrier-silex
            vomi
par la gueule du serpent de la mangrove

through some of the words obsessing a torpor
and the welcome and awakening of each one of our hurts
i enunciate you   *words*
        FANON   *Superb*
you scratch the iron
you scratch the bars of the jail
you scratch the gaze of the torturer
flint warrior
            vomited
through the mangrove swamp serpent's snout

7

pour dire . . .

pour revitaliser le rugissement des phosphènes
le cœur creux des comètes

pour raviver le verso solaire des rêves
leur laitance
pour activer le frais flux des sèves la mémoire des silicates

colère des peuples débouché des Dieux leur ressaut
patienter le mot son or son orle
jusqu'à ignivome
sa bouche

7 ✓

in order to speak . . .

in order to revitalize the roaring of phosphenes
the hollow core of comets

in order to revive the solar verso of dreams
their roe
in order to activate the fresh flux of saps the memory of
    silicates

anger of the people outlet of the Gods their recoil
be patient the word its or its orle
to the point of firevomiting
its mouth

8

il y a les archanges du Grand Temps
qui sont les ambassadeurs essaimés de la Turbulence
on les avait crus jusqu'à présent prisonniers
d'un protocole sidéral
les voici accueillis sur le seuil des cases
par de grandes attentes en armure verte
les mêmes qui les ont fascinés de très loin
de leurs calmes yeux insomniaques à peine
rougis du cheminement d'un lendemain naissant

il y a aussi les capteurs solaires du désir
de nuit je les braque: ce sont mots
que j'entasse dans mes réserves
et dont l'énergie est à dispenser
aux temps froids des peuples
(ni drèches ni bagasses
poussez les feux précieux
il serait immoral
que les dévoltages du Temps
puissent résister aux survoltages du Sang)

dévaler dur
contourner aux lieux choisis de la gravité historique
quelques abîmes
revenir dans cette mangrove buisson de lèvres
et de mancenilliers

8

there are archangels of Great Time
who are ambassadors swarmed out of Turbulence
up to now they were believed to be prisoners
of a sidereal protocol
here they are welcomed at the doorstep of the shacks
by great expectations in green armor
the very ones who fascinated them from far away
with their calm sleepless eyes barely
reddened by the approach of a nascent tomorrow

there are also solar captors of desire
at night i pull a gun on them: they are the words
that i amass in my stockroom
whose energy is to be dispersed
during the cold weather of people
(neither draff nor bagasse
let the precious fires be stirred
it would be immoral
for the voltage reductions of Time
to be able to resist the voltage boosting of the Blood)

to come down hard
to pass around a few abysses
in places chosen for their historical weight
to come back to this mangrove swamp a bush of lips
of manchineels

encore toujours encore
c'est la rancœur des mots qui nous guide
leur odeur perfide
      (bavure faite de l'intime amitié de nos blessures
      comme leur rage n'était que la recristallisation
      d'incendies de ghettos)
le mot oiseau-tonnerre
le mot dragon-du-lac
le mot strix
le mot lémure
le mot touaou
        couresses que j'allaite

ils me reniflent et viennent
      à l'heure
         au lieu
            à moi
pour être
s'y faisant un groin la griffe
           le bec
l'abandon est plus loin au crépuscule sur le sable
      mal sade et fade
et l'atroce rancune de salive ravalée du ressac

again and ever again
it is the rancor of words that guides us
their perfidious smell
        (slime made from the intimate friendship of our wounds
        just as their rage was nothing but the recrystallization
        of burning ghettos)
the word thunderbird
the word dragon-of-the-lake
the word Strix
the word lemur
the word touaou   *
        couresses that I nurse   *

they sniff at me and come
        on time
                to the place
                        to me
in order to be
there making a snout the claw
                        the beak
giving up comes later at dusk on the sand
                sapid and insipid evil
the dreadful resentment of saliva reswallowed by the surf

il n'est pas toujours bon de barboter dans le premier marigot
   venu
il n'est pas toujours bon de se vautrer dans la torpeur des
   mornes
il n'est pas toujours bon de se perdre
dans la contemplation gnoséologique
au creux le plus fructueux des arbres généalogiques
(le risque étant de s'apercevoir que l'on s'est égaré au plus
   mauvais carrefour de l'évolution)
alors?
   je ne suis pas homme à toujours chanter Maré Maré
   le guerrier qui meurt que nul ne voit tomber
terre et eaux bave assez
            poitrail d'avril
            étrave
            cheval

9

mangrove swamp

it is not always a good idea to splash about in just any
    brackish pond
it is not always a good idea to wallow in the torpor of
    mornes
it is not always good to lose oneself
in gnoseological contemplation
at the most fruitful hollow of genealogical trees
(the risk being to realize that one went astray at the worst
    possible crossroad of evolution)
so?
    i'm not the kind of man who goes around singing Maré
        Maré   *
    the dying warrior no one sees fall
spews dirt and water aplenty
        april his breastplate
        stempost
        stallion

chanson de l'hippocampe

petit cheval hors du temps enfui
bravant les lès du vent et la vague et le sable turbulent
petit cheval
       dos cambré que salpêtre le vent
tête basse vers le cri des juments
petit cheval sans nageoire
             sans mémoire
débris de fin de course et sédition de continents
fier petit cheval têtu d'amours supputées
mal arrachés au sifflement des mares

un jour rétif
       nous t'enfourcherons

et tu galoperas petit cheval
sans peur
vrai dans le vent le sel et le varech

song of the sea horse

tiny horse escaped from time
braving the towpaths of wind and waves and turbulent sand
tiny horse
                arched back saltpetered by the wind
head low toward the cry of mares
tiny horse without fins
                without memory
debris from the end of the run and the sedition of continents
proud tiny horse stubborn from calculated loves
badly torn in the hiss of stagnant ponds

one restive day
                we will mount you

and away you'll gallop tiny horse
fearless
unerring in the wind the salt and the wrack

l'incapacité d'un dire ou de très réels chevaux hennissant
fatras d'écoute ~~Sail & liste~~
fatras de houles de criques d'herbes froissées
leur odeur seule transmission sûre de la vomissure

appels déchiquetés de conques sans appel
                    odeurs odeurs
                            sueurs
                                et
                            lueurs
poussière de rites de mythes
—mémoires mangées aux mites—
fou farfouillement de sources
parmi le bric à brac de terres qui s'éboulent
aux paysages-mirages
                    virage à l'habitude et
                            narquois
le grand air silencieux de la déchirure

wreckage

someone's impotent utterance or else very real horses
   neighing
a jumble of sails
a jumble of swells of coves of trampled grass
their smell the only sure transmittal of vomit

jagged appeals of conches without appeal
         smells smells
              sweatings
                and
                 glimmers
dust of rituals of myths
—moth-eaten memories—
insane ransacking of sources
amidst the bric-a-brac of lands crumbling
into mirage-scapes
             winging it and
                cunning
the silentious open air of the split

incidents de voyage:
        de la vermine
    un ordinaire de mouches
    un obsédant baiser de ravets
    là-haut de feuillage en feuillage
    l'armée des lunes lançant leurs vagues à l'assaut de quels
        singes
    attention dans les vallées
        le velours du détour
        se mesure à un désordre d'insectes abrutis flaque
de toute façon
        il n'est pas recommandé de se complaire aux haltes

typical . . .

incidents along the way:
                    vermin
          a typical quota of flies
          an obsessing kiss of cockroaches
     up there from frond to frond
     the army of moons launching waves to attack
          who knows what apes
     in the valleys beware
               the velvetings of the detour
               can be measured by a chaos of dazed bugs plash
in any case
               it is not recommended to indulge in breaks

mais vint l'odeur
  l'odeur dit.
    sobrement dit.
de goémon
  de sueur de nègres
  d'herbe
  de vesou
  de coutelas
  de mangle.
l'odeur dit
  c'est tout dire.
l'odeur n'est pas vide.
  l'odeur n'a pas de rides.

13 ★
(didn't mention
but good ore)

smell

but the smell came
  the smell spoke.
    soberly spoke.
of seaweed
  of niggers' sweat
  of grass
  of cane juice
  of cutlasses
  of mangrove fruit.
the smell spoke
  need one say more.
the smell is not hollow.
  the smell has no folds.

I4

la condition-mangrove

Le désespoir n'a pas de nom
une main agite mou le drapeau de toutes les redditions
c'est le grand anguillard qui nous fait signe
que les gentillesses sont hors de saison
On tourne en rond. Autour du pot.
Le pot au noir bien sûr.
Noire la mangrove reste un miroir.
Aussi une mangeoire.
La mangrove broie-tapie à part.
La mangrove respire. Méphitique. Vasard.
La tourbière serait bien pire.
(Ce n'est rien que du haut: mort à la base même portant
    beau)
Au contraire le fruit flotte le poisson grimpe aux arbres
On peut très bien survivre mou
en prenant assise sur la vase commensale
L'allure est des forêts.
La dodine
        celle du balancement des marées

the mangrove swamp syndrome

Despair has no name
a hand is waving the limp flag of all the surrenderings
it is the anguillard who indicates to us   eel (?)   *
that amenities are out of season
One beats around the bush. Around the pot.
The pitch pot of course.
Pitch black the mangrove swamp remains a mirror.
A manger as well. (where minals eat)
The mangrove swamp lurks-grinds on its own.
The mangrove swamp breathes. Mephitic. Mud-bottomed.
The peatbog would be much worse.
(A top, that's all there is: dead at the base in spite of its noble
     appearance)
On the contrary the fruit floats the fish climbs the trees   surrealista
It is quite possible to survive limp
by anchoring oneself in the commensal mud
The look is that of forests.
The lulling
          that of the swaying of tides

même tabac
cette grande balafre à mon ventre
ou ce fleuve en plein cœur
    seul réveil
la parole des ressauts
    mal débité ce sang
le courage n'est pas de remonter
le regard s'égare vers le bas aux vasières
que fixe seul hagard
poto-poto des Calabars
le pied des palétuviers

rivers are not impassive

same brawl
this big scar on my belly
or this river straight into my heart
sole arousal
the leap of indignation
poorly apportioned this blood
the courage is not to swim upstream
the eye drifts down to the mudholes
the Calabar poto-poto
sole haggard grippers of
the mangroves' base

rien que la masse de manœuvre de la torpeur à manœuvrer
rien que le jour des autres et leur séjour
rien que ce troupeau de douteux lézards qui reviennent
    plutôt gaiement
        du pâturage et leurs conciliabules infâmes
        aux découpes de bayous
        de mon sang méandre à mumbo-jumbo

rien que cette manière de laper chaque hasard de mon
    champ vital
        et de raréfier à dose l'ozone natal

rien que le déménagement de moi-même sous le rire bas
des malebêtes
rien que l'hégémonie du brouillard qu'atteste la nappe
qu'il s'est tirée
        sur la cendre des vies entraperçues de tours
            écroulées
        de désirs à peine mâchés puis recrachés (épaves qui
            m'absentent)

rien que du passé son bruit de lointaine canonnade dans le
    ciel
je ne le sais que trop
un visage à organiser
une journée à déminer
et toujours cette maldonne à franchir étape par étape
à charge pour moi d'inventer chaque point d'eau.

---

only the laborer's sledge of torpor to maneuver
only the present of others and their presence
only this herd of suspect lizards almost gaily coming back
       from the pasture and their ignominious secret
          meetings
       in the fretwork of the bayous
       of my blood a mumbo-jumbo meander

only this manner of lapping up each chance from my vital
  field
       and of rarifying my natal ozone dose by dose

only the moving out of the house of my self under the
  sniggering of hellhounds
only the hegemony of the fog attested by the blanket
that it pulled for itself
       over the ash of half-glimpsed lives of collapsed
         towers
       of desires barely chewed then spat out again
       (wreckage removing itself from me)

of the past only the boom of distant cannons in the sky
i know it only too well
a face to organize
a day to strip of its mines
and always this misdeal to negotiate step by step
stuck as i am with inventing each water hole.

---

pensées éboulis d'abris
rêves-boiteries
désirs segments de sarments
(une combinatoire qui s'excède)
rien de tout cela n'a la force d'aller bien loin
essoufflés
ce sont nos oiseaux tombant et retombant
alourdis par le sucroît de cendre des volcans

hors sens. hors coup. hors gamme.
à preuve les grands fagots de mots qui dans les coins
      s'écroulent.
rage. ravage. coup de chien. coup de tabac. coup pour rien.

autant tracer des signes magiques
sur un rocher
sur un galet
à l'intention des dieux d'en bas pour exercer
leur patience.

à vrai dire
j'ai le sentiment que j'ai perdu quelque chose:
une clef la clef
ou que je suis quelque chose de perdu
rejeté, forjeté
au juste par quels ancêtres?
inutile d'accuser la dérive génétique

vaille que vaille la retrouvaille

encore que le combat soit désormais avec le paysage
qui de temps en temps crève la torpeur des compitales
à petit coup d'un ressentiment douteux

debris

thoughts debris of shelters
dreams-limpings
desires segments of dry stems
(a combinative that exhausts itself)
nothing of all of this has the strength to go very far
winded
are our birds falling and refalling
weighed down by the excess of volcanic ash

out of sense. out of it. out of tune.
witness the thick bundles of words crumbling in the corners.
rage. ravage. squall. brawl. senseless blow.

might as well draw magic signs
on a rock
on a pebble
for the benefit of the gods down there to test
their patience.

to tell the truth
i have a hunch that i've lost something:
a key the key
or that i am something that has been lost
rejected, poorly-jutted
by which ancestors exactly?
useless to blame genetic drift

at any cost the grand reunion

even though the struggle from now on is with the landscape
which from time to time breaks the torpor of the Compitalia   *
with a little bit of dubious resentment

avec des bouts de ficelle
avec des rognures de bois
avec de tout tous les morceaux bas
avec les coups bas
avec des feuilles mortes ramassées à la pelle
avec des restants de draps
avec des lassos lacérés
avec des mailles forcées de cadène
avec des ossements de murènes
avec des fouets arrachés
avec des conques marines
avec des drapeaux et des tombes dépareillées
        par rhombes
        et trombes
te bâtir

18

link of the chain gang

with bits of string
with wood shavings
with anything all the cheap cuts
with low blows
with shovelfuls of dead leaves
with remnants of cloth
with lacerate lassos
with links snapped from the chain gang
with the bones of moray eels
with torn-away whips
with sea conches
with flags and tombs mismatched
     by whirlwinds
     and waterspouts
to build thee

19

j'ai guidé du troupeau
la longue transhumance

marcher à travers des sommeils de cyclones transportant
des villes somnambules dans leurs bras endoloris
croiser à mi-pente du saccage des quartiers entiers d'astres
    fourvoyés

marcher non sans entêtement à travers ce pays sans cartes
dont la décomposition périphérique aura épargné je présume
l'indubitable corps ou cœur sidéral

marcher sur la gueule pas tellement bien ourlée des volcans

marcher sur la fracture mal réduite des continents
(rien ne sert de parcourir la Grande Fosse
d'inspecter tous les croisements d'examiner les ossements
de parent à parent il manque toujours un maillon)

marcher en se disant qu'il est impossible
que la surtension atmosphérique
captée par les oiseaux parafoudres
n'ait pas été retransmise quelque part
en tout cas quelque part un homme est qui l'attend
il s'est arrêté un moment
le temps pour un nuage d'installer une belle parade de
    trochilidés
l'éventail à n'en pas douter à éventer d'or jeune
la partie la plus plutonique d'une pépite qui n'est pas
autre chose que le ventre flammé d'un beau temps récessif

i guided the long transhumance
of the herd

to walk across the slumbers of cyclones that carry
somnambulant cities in their sore arms
halfway up the hill of the plundering to come across whole
    districts of lost stars

to walk not without stubbornness across this uncharted land
whose peripheral decomposition will have spared I presume
    the indubitable sidereal body or heart

to walk on the rather clumsily rimmed muzzles of volcanoes

to walk on the poorly set fractures of continents
(no use in traveling the Great Trench
in inspecting all the crossings in examining all the bones
from parent to parent there is always one link missing)

to walk telling oneself that it is impossible
that the atmospheric overpressure
captured by thunder-rod birds
was not retransmitted somewhere
at any rate somewhere a man exists waiting for it
he stopped for a moment
the time it takes for a cloud to organize a beautiful parade
    of trochilidae
the fan assuredly to fan with new gold
the most plutonic part of a nugget that is none other than
the flambé belly of receding fair weather

pour me distraire
vais-je prendre en charge encore cette journée?
pour me distraire à mon ordinaire je bâtis.
quelques chicots—il ne reste plus que cela de dur—
quelques oiseaux au-dessus de la merde
quelques crachats

et c'est une ville harassée de nuages
que mégote goguenard
le museau d'un volcan inattentif.

20

a day

to amuse myself
shall i again take charge of this day?
to amuse myself as usual i build.
a few stumps of teeth—the only hard thing left to me—
a few birds over shit
some spittle

and it is a town harassed by clouds
that hangs, facetiously, like a fag end,
from the muzzle of an oblivious volcano.

soleil safre

au pied de volcans bègues
plus tôt que le petit brouillard violet qui monte
de ma fièvre je suis assis au milieu d'une cour
horologue de trois siècles accumulés en fientes de
   chauves-souris
sous la fausse espérance de doux grigris

déjà hurlant d'âme chienne
et portant les vraies chaînes
ai-je mille de mes cœurs rendu
pour celui d'aujourd'hui qui
très fort
à la gorge nous remonte
parakimomène de hauts royaumes amers
moi
soleil safre

21

at the foot of stammering volcanoes
earlier than the little violet fog arising from my fever
i am sitting in the middle of a courtyard
a horologer of three centuries accumulated in bat droppings
under the false hope of sweet grigris

already howling from a bitch soul
and carrying the true shackles
i have exchanged a thousand of my hearts
for the one today that
powerfully
rises in our throat
parakinesized by lofty bitter kingdoms   *
i
zaffer sun

la relance ici se fait
par le vent qui d'Afrique vient
par la poussière d'alizé
par la vertu de l'écume
et la force de la terre

nu
l'essentiel est de sentir nu
de penser nu
        la poussière d'alizé
        la vertu de l'écume
        et la force de la terre
la relance ici se fait par l'influx
plus encore que par l'afflux
        la relance
            se fait
                algue laminaire

algae

the resurgence takes place here
through wind born in Africa
through the dust of trade winds
through the properties of spume
and the strength of the earth

naked
.the main thing is to sniff nakedly
to think nakedly
       the dust of trade winds
      the properties of spume
      and the strength of the earth
the resurgence here takes place through influx
even more than through afflux   *a flow toward*
        the resurgence   *a point*
          takes place
           laminarian alga

le mot est père des saints
le mot est mère des saints
avec le mot *couresse* on peut traverser un fleuve peuplé de
    caïmans
il m'arrive de dessiner un mot sur le sol
avec un mot frais on peut traverser le désert d'une journée
il y a des mots bâton-de-nage pour écarter les squales
il y a des mots iguanes
il y a des mots subtils ce sont des mots phasmes
il y a des mots d'ombre avec des réveils en colère d'étincelles
il y a des mots Shango
il m'arrive de nager de ruse sur le dos d'un mot dauphin

prince
+ dolphin

macumba word

the word is the father of the saints
the word is the mother of the saints
with the word *couresse* one can cross a river swarming with
    caimans
sometimes i trace a word in the dirt
with a fresh word one can cross the desert in a single day
there are swim-stick words for pushing away sharks
there are iguana words
there are subtle words those are stick-insect words
there are shadow words that awake sparking with anger
there are Shango words   *
sometimes i even sneak a swim on the back of a dolphin
    word

ça ne se meuble pas
               c'est creux
ça ne s'arrache pas
               ce n'est pas une fleur
ça s'effilocherait plutôt
               étoupe pour étouffer les cris
(s'avachissant ferme)
ça se traverse
             —pas forcément à toute vitesse—
tunnel
ça se gravit aussi en montagne
glu
    le plus souvent ça se rampe

24

that, the hollow

that is unfurnishable
                     it is hollow
that is unpluckable
                     it is not a flower
that is shreddable rather
                     stuffing for stifling screams
(slackening for sure)
that is crossable
                     —not necessarily at full speed—
a tunnel
that is also climbable like a mountain
birdlime
                     in most cases that is crawlable

les nuits de par ici sont des nuits sans façon
elles sont toujours en papillotes
elles ne sont pas sans force
même si elles sont sans mains pour brandir le coutelas
mais force reste à la loi—à l'angoisse
la nuit ici
      descend
         de grillons en grenouilles
      doucement les pieds nus
      en bas
      un gosier de coq patiente
      pour cueillir la giclée
ce n'est pas toujours de la cellule de gestion de la
    castastrophe
que la journée téméraire fait part de sa propre naissance

nights

the nights over here are not worth writing home about
they're always in their curlers
they are not without strength
even if they lack hands to brandish the cutlass
but the law carries the day—or anxiety does
the night here
       comes down
           from crickets to frogs
       softly barefoot
       down here
       a rooster's throat patiently awaits
       the harvesting of his spurt
it is not always from the management cell of the catastrophe
that the temeritous day announces its own birth

que la sève ne s'égare pas aux fausses pistes
on s'étonne
moins (vomie de flammes)
que la chimère éteinte se traînaille en limace
Ravine Ravine
être ravin du monde
ce n'est pas se complaire à n'être
que le clandestin Cédron de toute la vermoulure
mauvais ange
   cœur trop tard débarqué
mauvais ange
   cœur trop mal embarqué
la force de mon soleil s'inquiète de la capacité
d'une journée d'homme

don't be taken in

that sap does not stray onto the wrong trails
is less surprising
than (vomited by flames)
the extinguished chimera dragging itself sluglike
Ravine Ravine
to be the ravine of the world
does not mean indulging in being nothing more
than the clandestine Kedron of all the worm dust
evil angel
          heart disembarked too soon
evil angel
          heart embarked too awkwardly
the strength of my sun worries about the capacity
of a man's day

sa part du soleil?
ses caprices ne sont pas sans rigueur
parfois il se cache la tête dans un sac de cendres
c'est là sa colère
parfois exposé
au vol bleu des heures tournoyant au-dessus de sa tête
c'est qu'il médite
il sait aussi sauter
parfois il se ronge
et lance à l'horizon une furie de galles
brandissant leur sexe sanglant
parfois il se peigne avec des dents de lémurien
parfois c'est un rien un fantôme—le mien—

pirate guet-apens de remords
le Soleil n'est pas là en intrus

pirate

his share of the sun?
his whims are not without rigor
sometimes he hides his head in a bag of ashes
that's how he shows anger
sometimes exposed
to the blue flight of hours hovering over his head
which means he meditates
he also knows how to leap
sometimes he eats his heart out
and hurls toward the horizon a fury of galls
brandishing their bloodied penises
sometimes he combs his hair with lemur teeth
sometimes he is a nothing a ghost—mine—

pirate ambush of remorse
the Sun is not here as an intruder

le verra-t-on enfin endosser sa propre force
le verra-t-on coup de cœur de l'éclair
sur la masse fade du faubourg
il pensa l'épaisseur de la nuit
il pensa longue
        longue
la longue moustache longue de l'incurable pacarana
il pensa la logique de l'outrage
alors il dit la pierre plus précieuse que la lumière

l'eau se trempant de feuilles vertes
il plut l'approche d'une équinoxe

stone

shall we finally see him endorse his own strength
shall we see him a stroke at the heart of lightning
over the tasteless mass of the suburb
he pondered the thickness of the night
he pondered long
                    long
the long long moustache of the incurable paca-rana
he pondered the logic of the outrage
then he spoke the stone more precious than light

the water soaking with green leaves
there rained the approach of an equinox

sans cette colère c'est clair
il ne s'agirait plus que d'une douceâtre fiente de malfini
mal dilué par les eaux

vomi des terres
je salue le vieux lion et son courroux de pierres

dans ce paysage
     —éclairage d'une rémanence—
       igitur
     non.
       solvitur

solvitur . . .

without this anger it is clear
we would be talking about nothing more than the sweetish
   droppings of the malfini   *
poorly diluted by the waters

vomit of lands
i salute the old lion and his stony wrath

in this landscape
       —afterglow of a remanence—
         igitur
       no.
         solvitur

le surplus
      je l'avais distribué aux rides des chemins
      à l'acharnement des ravins
les forces ne s'épuisent pas si vite
quand on n'en est que le dépositaire fragile.
qui combien aux prix de quels hasards
les avaient amassées?

      un signe
      un rien
      une lueur au bas du ciel
      une flamme née du sol
      un tremblement de l'air
      le signe que rien n'est mort

je hurlais:
      vous n'avez pas le droit de laisser couper
      le chemin de la transmission

je hurlais:
      la bouffonnerie des neurones
      suffit à mettre hors de cause l'état de la caldeira

je hurlais au violent éclatement

cependant le temps me serpait dur
jusqu'à la racine intacte.

30

the surplus
    i had shed it into the ruts of the roads
    into the stubbornness of gullies
forces are not exhausted that quickly
when one is only their puny trustee.
who how many at the cost of what risks
had amassed them?

    a sign
    a nothing
    a glimmer in the depths of the sky
    a flame born of the ground
    a quivering of the air
    the sign that nothing is dead

i was screaming:
    you have no right to allow
    the transmission channel to be cut

i was screaming:
  the buffoonery of neurons
  suffices to exonerate the state of the caldera

i was screaming as if to violently explode

meanwhile time was hacking at me harshly
down to my intact root.

---

la suractivation des terres
qui n'est pas autre chose que la compensation
de la lenteur des sangs
je la retrouve dieu merci
dans ce délire compliqué de roches mal roulées
que l'on a trop vite fait de qualifier d'infernal
comme si l'enfer n'était pas
précisé par cette foutaise solaire assez peu ingénue.

arrêtez le gâchis
 on a peine à s'imaginer que tout est perdu
 puisque l'énergie des cendres est toujours là
 et souffle de temps en temps
 à travers les décombres.

slowness

the hyperactivating of the lands
which is nothing else than a compensation
for the slowness of blood
i find it again thank god
in this complicated delirium of weirdly shaped rocks
that one too quickly calls infernal
as if hell were not
revealed by this rather disingenuous solar rubbish.

stop the mess
      it is hard to imagine all is lost
      since the energy of ashes is still here
      and blows from time to time
              through the debris.

connaissance des mornes

les mornes ne sont pas une convulsion d'oiseaux géants
étouffés par le vent

les mornes ne sont pas un désespoir de cétacés
condamnés à l'échouage

les mornes ne sont pas une culbute de taureaux
s'effondrant sous le coup de poignard de Mithra

mornes
        mornes mâles
        mornes femelles
tendres cous d'animaux aussi frémissant au repos
mornes miens
        mornes témoins
effort
        je n'ai pas méconnu
récade ou torche trop précoce
votre hache plantée claire
dans le cœur sec des sommeils et la stupeur des sables

knowledge of mornes

the mornes are not a convulsion of giant birds
smothered by the wind

the mornes are not the despair of cetaceans
condemned to running aground

the mornes are not a somersault of bulls
collapsing under the thrust of Mithra's dagger

mornes
    male mornes
    female mornes
the tender necks of animals as well, trembling while resting
my own mornes
    witness mornes
effort
    i did not ignore
recado or too precocious torch   *
your ax planted clearly
in the dry heart of slumbers and the stupor of sands

entre deux bouffées d'oiseaux personnels
l'hébétude et la route à mi-côte
gluante d'un sperme cétacé
le malheur au loin de l'homme se mesure aux silences de ce
    volcan qui survit en clepsydre aux débris de son courage
la chose à souhaiter c'est le vent
je me mets sur le passage du vent
pollens ou aile je me veux piège à vent
        jouet du vent
        guette du vent méprisant
ah! cette route à mi-côte et son surplus solide
j'attends
        j'attends
           le vent

33

torpor of history

between two puffs of familiar birds
the stupor and the road halfway up
gluey with cetacean sperm
calamity at a distance from man can be measured by the
    silences of this volcano that like a clepsydra survived the
    debris of its courage
the thing to wish for is wind
i place myself on the passage of the wind
pollen or wing i wish myself a wind trap
        a toy for the wind
        a watchtower for the contemptuous wind
ah! that road halfway up and its solid surplus
i'm awaiting
        awaiting
            the wind

34

sans instance ce sang

toujours, pas tant vif que beau, l'air, sauf ce souffle que nous pousse la vraie terre, langue bleue et fidèle précation d'ancêtres

je vois, descendant les marches de la montagne, dans un dénouement que rendent vaste les papillons, les reines qui sortent en grande dentelle de leurs prisons votives

elles s'étonnent à bon droit que le feu central consente à se laisser confiner pour combien de temps encore dans la bonne conscience des châteaux de termitières qu'il s'est édifiés un peu partout

quant au Soleil, un Soleil de frontière
il cherche le poteau-mitan autour duquel faire tourner pour qu'enfin l'avenir commence

ces saisons insaisissables ce ciel sans cil et sans instance ce sang

this appeal-prohibited blood

always, less lively than beautiful, the air, save for this breath exhaled for us by the true earth, a blue tongue and a faithful precation of ancestors

i see, descending the mountain steps, in a denouement greatly magnified by butterflies, the queens emerging from their votive prisons in an endless lace

they are rightly astonished that the central fire consents to let itself be confined for how much longer in the good conscience of the termitarium castles that it built for itself here and there

as for the Sun, a frontier Sun
it is seeking the center post around which to rotate so that the future may finally commence

these unseizable seasons this eyelash-denied sky and this appeal-prohibited blood

mémoire honorant le paysage
décompte
le foyer nourrit à s'y méprendre l'équité d'un cratère
un souvenir de peau très douce ne s'interdit pas
aux paumes d'un automne

hearth . . .

memory honoring the landscape
an abatement
the hearth nurtures most convincingly the equity of a crater
a recollection of very soft skin is not out of the question
in the palms of an autumn

la Justice écoute aux portes de la Beauté

une envolée
s'immobilise en fougères arborescentes
et gracieusement salue en inclinant leurs ombrelles
à peine frémissantes

une saison plus bas la Reine met pied à terre
elle revient dans la confidence des éléments
d'une cérémonie où elle a présidé
à l'opalisation du désastre et à la transmutation des
    silicates

très simplement elle dépose sa couronne
qui n'est paradoxalement qu'une guirlande de fleurs
de técomarias très intenses

et nous fait les honneurs de son palais paraquatique
gardé de varans de pierre

drapeaux draperies scories pêle-mêle de fanfares
et de sèves
par feu par cendres
        sachons:

la tache de beauté fait ici sa tâche
elle sonne somme exige l'obscur déjà
et que la fête soit refaite
et que rayonne justice
en vérité la plus haute

36

Justice listens at the gates of Beauty

a flight
pauses in the tree ferns
and bows gracefully bending the barely quivering
sunshades

a season further down the Queen dismounts
returning in complicity with the elements
from a ceremony where she presided over
the opalization of disaster and the transmutation of
    silicates

very simply she puts down her crown
which is paradoxically no more than a wreath of very intense
tecoma flowers

and does us the honors of her paraquatic palace
guarded by stone varans

flags hangings scoriae hubbub of fanfares
and of sap
through fire through ashes
    let us keep in mind:

the taint in beauty here performs her task
she rings for summons demands the obscure already
that the feast be restored
that justice beam
indeed above everything

---

le noir pavillon claquant au vent toujours barbaresque
les feux à mi-chemin entre la lumière biologique la plus
    pressante et la sérénité des constellations
la mise en contact qui ne peut se faire qu'à partir de très
    rares macles de minéraux

Cimarrone sans doute

(le pan de ce visage qui dans l'écume d'un silence
tombe avec des biseautés de mangue)
tellement à la faveur d'oiseaux
dont l'office est à force de pollen
de corriger les bévues des Erinnyes et le raide vin des
    murènes

37

a freedom in passage

the Jolly Roger flapping in the ever Barbary wind
the lights halfway between the most pressing biological
    clarity and the serenity of the constellations
the connecting that can only take place using very rare
    mineral macles

Cimarron undoubtedly

(the section of this face that in the frothing of a silence
falls amidst mangolike bevelings)
helped so much by birds
whose mission is by dint of pollen
to correct the Erinyes' blunders and the stiff wine of moray
    eels

inventaire de cayes

(à siffler sur la route)

beaux
      beaux
            Caraïbos
quelle volière
            quels oiseaux
cadavres de bêtes
            cadavres d'oiseaux
autour du marécage
            moins moins beau le marécage
            moins beau que le Maracaïbo

beaux beaux les piranhas
            beaux beaux les stymphanos
quant à vous sifflez sifflez
(encore un mauvais coup d'Eshu)

            boca del Toro
            boca del Drago

chanson chanson de cage
adieu volière
            adieu oiseaux

38

inventory of reefs

(for whistling on the road)

so comely
         so comely
                 Caribbees
what aviaries
         what cagelings

around the bog
              beast cadavers
bird cadavers
         much less comely the bog
         less comely than the Maracaibo

so comely so comely—piranhas
              so comely so comely—stymphalians
as for you—keep whistling
(the latest dirty trick of Eshu)

               boca del Toro
              boca del Drago

chanson chanson of the cage
adieu aviary
         cagelings adieu

à valoir . . .

contrefaisances
ceux qui de leur pierre à regards assassinent
les plus exotiques printemps
les saccageurs convergents
des plus somptueuses parures des sporanges des plasmodes
au guachamaca dont même la fumée empoisonne
blanche caresse de ce fond de ravin
nuages
traîneurs des savates éculées du soleil dans le ciel des peuples
    résignés
oiseaux débris de vol
siffle-sève sévères
il n'est pas que vous n'ayez pas compris sa pompe et mon
attente mesurée au déclic d'horloge du serpent-minute
l'explosion
après quoi il est convenu d'apprécier que
vient la poigne rude du petit matin attentatoire de planter
    au faîte d'un poui le plus oublié
sa parure de feu
     son dolman de sang
         son drapeau de rage et de renouveau

39

to be deducted . . .

apings
those who with their gazestone assassinate
the most exotic springtimes
pillagers converging
from the most sumptuous adornments of the spore cases of
   plasmodia to the guachamaca whose smoke alone poisons,
a white caress of this gully's depth
clouds
draggers of the sun's worn-down heels in the sky of resigned
   peoples
birds debris of flight
severe sap-sippers
it is not that you have not understood its pomp and my
   waiting measured by the clock click of the serpent-minute
the explosion
after which it is proper to appreciate that
the brutal fist of the terrorist crack of dawn has just planted
   at the top of the most forgotten poui   *
its ornament of fire
      its dolman of blood
            its flag of rage and renewal

conspiration . . .

les pierres leur furent sans mœlle prison d'escargots
et passion de pagures les insectes au bâillon
cervelle brûlée dans le creux des métaux.

prirent en haine leur démon
troquèrent contre muids fades sans toxines
les pieuvres de leur sang et leurs tendres bras longs.

dénoncèrent les pactes même les plus millénaires
cependant que s'installa le crémeux sourire blanc.

qui, qui donc envoyait le grand froid, loas?
celui du sexe, celui de l'arbre à pain et de la pierre
et de la sève qui fut jadis rouissage de colibris?

en tout cas, je suis, moi, de la plus longue marche
et je ne déteste pas qu'on se le redise
j'ai noué contre la toute-puissance glaciation
la conspiration avouée
de l'ours noir et de l'albatros des Galapagos
du manate et de l'agami trompette, de l'eau de mer
et des cratères

exarque des avalanches j'ai convoqué pour toutes
utiles
représailles
pour le rebrousse-temps et le rebrousse-sang
tous les réchauffeurs solaires rolliers et tisserins.

40

conspiracy . . .

for them the stones were without marrow a snail-prison
and gagged insects the passion of hermit-crabs
a fried brain in the pit of metals.

they conceived their demon in hate
traded for bland poisonless hogsheads
the octopuses of their blood and their tender long arms.

denounced even the most ancient of pacts
while the creamy white smile settled in.

who, who then was sending the great cold, loas?
that of the sex, that of the breadfruit tree and of the stone
and of the sap that used to be hummingbird retting?

at any rate, in my case, i am from the longest of marches
and i rather like people telling one another about it
against the all-powerful glaciation i knotted
the avowed conspiracy
of the black bear and the Galapagos albatross
of the manatee and the trumpeter agami, of seawater
and craters

an exarch of avalanches i convoked for all
necessary
reprisals
for brushing against the nap of time and blood
all the solar heaters roller and weaver birds.

169

quant au sang qui est de mêche
nous prendrons par les bédières
et nous passerons au col du Désastre
—impudence et virulence—les mots lassos

on a souvent vu une giclée d'eau vivante
faire tomber la tête de la Bête.

as for the blood that's in collusion
we will follow the way of the glacial streams
and will fling the lasso words
—impudence and virulence—through the col of Disaster

it will not be the first time that a jet of living water
topples the head of the Beast.

je les reconnais
               l'odeur le souffle le rien
contact de mufles
             états d'âme
                  états-aoûtats
ma terreur est de voir déboucher l'escouade des sans nom
ceux-là travaillent dans le furtif le soir la soie
lapant souriant l'évidence d'une chaleur—leur proie

ou bien selon les besoins de leur saison grignotant le coprah
non exsangue, sifflant chaque goutte à travers la paille de
chaque seconde, coupant les muscles au fil du silence,
le Monstre.

il y a longtemps que j'ai dressé la carte de ses subterfuges
mais il ne sait pas qu'au moment du répit
le sortant de ma poitrine j'en ferai un collier
de fleurs voraces
et je danse Monstre je danse
dans la résine des mots et paré d'exuvies
nu.

ma défense: gravés par la dent du sable sur le galet
—c'est mon cœur arraché des mains du séisme—
LE CHIFFRE

monsters

i recognize them
      the smell the breath a mere nothing
contact of muzzles
        states of mind
           states-of-mites
my terror is in seeing the squad of the nameless emerge
they work by stealth by night in silk
lapping up smiling the evidence of a warmth—their prey

or else depending on seasonal need nibbling nonanaemic
   copra,
swigging each drop through the straw of each second,
   cutting
the muscles on the blade of silence,
the Monster.

it was long ago that i drew up a map of its subterfuges
but it does not know that during a lull
pulling it out of my chest i will turn it into a necklace
of voracious flowers
and i dance Monster i dance
in the resin of words, decorated in exuvia
naked.

my defense: engraved by a tooth of sand on the pebble
—it is my heart torn from the hands of the earthquake—
THE CIPHER

il m'arrive de le perdre
des semaines
c'est ma créature mais rebelle

un petit mot couresse
un petit mot crabe-c'est-ma-faute
un petit mot pétale de feu
un petit mot pétrel plongeur
un petit mot saxifrage de tombeaux

petit mot qui m'atteste je te lance tiaulé
dans le temps et les confins
assistant à ton assaut sévère
spectral et saccadé
et de mon sang luciole parmi les lucioles

internuncio

off and on i lose it
for weeks
it is my creature but a rebellious one

a little word coumesse
a little word through-my-fault crab
a little word petal of fire
a little word diving petrel
a little word tomb saxifrage

little word that gives evidence of me i throw you trillando
into time and the outer reaches
witnessing your severe assault
spectral and spasmodic
and of my own blood a firefly among the fireflies

reprenons
      l'utile chemin patient
      plus bas que les racines le chemin de la graine
le miracle sommaire bat des cartes
mais il n'y a pas de miracle
seule la force des graines
selon leur entêtement à mûrir

parler c'est accompagner la graine
jusqu'au noir secret des nombres

43

path

let us take up again
       the useful patient path
       lower than roots the path of seed
the summary miracle shuffles the deck
but there is no miracle
only the strength of seeds
depending on their stubbornness to ripen

to speak is to go with the seed
all the way to the black secret of numbers

les combinaisons les plus variées nous ramènent toujours
à la version d'un venin de feu ou même
à la vermine des métaux
l'avenir étant toujour scellé aux armes de la rouille
et du cachet des cendres
le décompte des décombres n'est jamais terminé.

44

venom version

the most varied combinations always bring us back
to the version of a fiery venom or even
to the vermin of metals
the future always being sealed with blazons of rust
and with the impress of ashes
the breakdown of debris takes forever

il pensa à la logique des dents du marécage
il pensa au plomb fondu dans la gorge de la Chimère
il pensa à une morgue de becs dans le mouroir des coraux
il pensa à la prorogation sans limites à travers
les plages du temps
de la querelle séculaire
(le temps d'une éclipse d'âme il y eut en travers
de moi-même la passion d'un piton)
il pensa à un trottinement de souris dans le palais d'une âme
    royale
il pensa à la voix de chiourme étranglée d'une chanson
puis par la halte sans âme d'un troupeau
à un isolat de limaces de mer coiffées de leur casque à venin

ainsi
      toute nostalgie
                à l'abîme
                      roule

45 ⌐

he pondered the logic of the swamp's teeth
he pondered the molten lead in the Chimera's throat
he pondered a morgue of beaks in the coral dump for the
    dying
he pondered the boundless extension
of the century-old quarrel
across the beaches of time
(in the time it took a soul to vanish there went
through me the passion of a piton)
he pondered a mouse pitter-pattering through the palace
    of a royal soul
he pondered the voice of a galley slave strangled by a song
then by the soulless halt of a herd
an isolate of sea slugs coiffed with venom helmets

thus
    all nostalgia
                rolls
                        into the abyss

46

il faut savoir traverser toute l'étendue du sang
sans être happé par les dents de dragon
d'un rêve de trahison

il faut savoir traverser toute l'épaisseur du sang
avec trois voyelles de fraîche eau
anxieusement renouvelée par l'oriflamme
toujours à reconsidérer d'une chaîne à briser

il faut savoir traverser le défilé nocturne
avec pour contrebande le reflet du dernier pain de singe
arraché au dernier baobab

il faut savoir longer sans défaillance cette falaise
d'où le pied de Scyrron nourrit d'un filet
de chairs fades une émeute de tortues

moins difficile en vérité moins difficile
que de supporter le saccage du grand cœur des saisons
soleil étourdiment distribué aux vers luisants
en brûlant en sang pur une attente incrédule

pillage

one must know how to cross the entire expanse of blood
without being snapped up by the dragon teeth
of a dream of treason

one must know how to cross the entire width of the blood
with three vowels of fresh water
anxiously renewed by the oriflamme
always to be reconsidered of a chain to be broken

one must know how to pass through the nocturnal gorge
smuggling only the reflection of the last monkey bread
torn from the last baobab

one must know how to unflinchingly edge along that cliff
from which Sciron's foot fed rioting turtles
a filet of tasteless flesh

not as difficult not as difficult indeed
as enduring the pillage of the great heart of the seasons
a sun thoughtlessly distributed to glowworms
while burning an incredulous expectation in pure blood

47

quelques traces d'érosion
des habitudes de gestes (produits de corrosion)
                                    les silences
des souvenirs aussi raz-de-marée
le chant profond du jamais refermé
impact et longue maturation de mangrove

sourde la sape
                toujours différé l'assaut
il est permis de jouer les rites du naufrage
(à situer quelque part entre allusion et illusion
la signature douloureuse d'un oiseau
sous les alphabets incompréhensibles du moment)

je ne saurai jamais premières d'un message
quelles paroles forcèrent ma gorge
ni quel effort rugina ma langue
que me reste-t-il ce jour sinon penser
qu'à la face du destin à l'avance j'éructai une vie
j'ai tiré au sort mes ancêtres une terre plénière
mais qui blesse qui mutile
tout ce qui abâtardit le fier regard
ou plus lente
ou plus riche
                la curée urubu ou le rostre zopilote
j'ai eu je garde j'ai
                le libre choix de mes ennemis

Couchant fantôme si s'y allume le mien
parole grand duc tu planeras ce cri à sa gueule d'anubis

47

a few traces of erosion
gestural habits (products of corrosion)
                    the silences
recollections also tidal waves
the deep song of the never reclosed
impact and a lengthy mangrove swamp maturation

mute the undermining
                the assault always deferred
one is permitted to perform the rites of shipwreck
(to be located somewhere between allusion and illusion
the painful signature of a bird
under the incomprehensible alphabets of the moment)

i will never know which words
—the first in a message—broke through my throat
nor what effort scaled my tongue
what do i have left today except to ponder
that in the face of destiny in advance i belched a life
i drew lots for my ancestors for a plenary earth
but one that wounds that mutilates
anything that bastardizes a proud gaze
or slower
or richer
                the urubu quarry or zopilote rostrum   *
i have had i keep i have
                a free choice of enemies

Phantom sunset if my own ignites there
eagle owl word you will plane this cry from its
    Anubis snout

48

crevasses

Ich steige schon dreihundert Jahr,
Und kann den Gipfel nicht erreichen.
Goethe, *Faust*
Je grimpe depuis trois cents ans
et ne puis atteindre le sommet.

La sombre épellation établit sa loi: . . . Ure . . . Usure! Barbarie . . . Blessure! Le Temps, lui, connaît le blason et démasque à temps son mufle forban. Précisément. Inutile que l'on se donne un quelconque signal. La route est de cervelle toujours libre.

On a toute licence: on avance, on pénètre dans le taillis, dans le fouillis. Tel est bien le piège.

Comme de juste, on s'empêtre dans les galaxies de limaille de semailles accumulées en conglomérats de madrépores: traces et rémanences. On marche à quatre pattes. On se dépêtre. Courbé toujours mais avançant. Allongées de récifs encapuchonnés de paquets rescapés de serpents fer-de-lance (à identifier d'ailleurs).

Pêle-mêle de silice, des traînées, de menées sournoises d'algues à déjouer, toute une cartoucherie clandestine, une musserie innommable, du décrochez-moi-ça antédiluvien et pouacre.

On tourne en rond. La naïveté est d'attendre qu'une voix, je dis bien qu'une voie vous dise: *par ici la sortie!* N'existe que le nœud. Nœud sur nœud. Pas d'embouchure.

La technique du pont de lianes sur l'abîme croupissant est trop compliquée. Oubliée depuis longtemps.

Longtemps une crevasse creusera et, déjà, ronge.

Crevasse. Cloportes. Enjamber? A quoi bon?

Moi qui rêvais autrefois d'une écriture belle de rage!

Crevasse j'aurai tenté.

---

1 8 6

48

Ich steige schon dreihundert Jahr,
Und kann den Gipfel nicht erreichen.
Goethe, *Faust*
I've been climbing for three hundred years
and I can't reach the summit.

Saturnine spelling establishes its law: Urus . . . Usury! Barbary . . . Bleeding! Time, he knows the blazon and unmasks his buccaneer's muzzle just in time. Precisely. No point in giving oneself any signal. The road in the brain is always open. One has complete license: one advances, one penetrates the underbrush, the tangle. That precisely is the trap.

As expected, one gets entangled in the galaxies of filings of sowings accumulated in the madrepore conglomerates: traces and vestiges. One walks on all fours. One extricates oneself. Still bent over but advancing. Length of reefs hooded with escaped packets of fer-de-lances (to be identified, by the way).

Hodgepodge of flint, trails, sneaky seaweed schemes to be avoided, a complete clandestine armory, an unnameable cache, an antediluvian and filthy flea market.

One turns in circles. Naiveté consists in waiting for a voice, a voice, i repeat, telling you: *the exit's over here!* Only the knot exists. Knot upon knot. No opening.

The technique of the liana bridge over the rotting abyss is too complicated. Long forgotten.

For a long time a crevasse will hollow out and, already, it's corroding.

Crevasse. Sowbugs. To step over? What's the use?

I who used to dream of a writing dazzling with rage!

Crevasse i will have attempted.

je croise mon squelette
qu'une faveur de fourmis manians porte à sa demeure
(tronc de baobab ou contrefort de fromager)
il va sans dire que j'ai eu soin de ma parole
elle s'est blottie au cœur d'un nid de lianes
noyau ardent d'un hérisson végétal
c'est que je l'ai instruite depuis longtemps
à jouer avec le feu entre les feux
et à porter l'ultime goutte d'eau sauvée
à une quelconque des lointaines ramifications du soleil
soleil sommeil
quand j'entendrai les premières caravanes de la sève passer
peinant vers les printemps
être dispos encore

vers un retard d'îles éteintes et d'assoupis volcans

49

i come across my skeleton
which a ribbon of fire ants is carrying to its dwelling
(a baobab trunk or a bombax buttress)
it goes without saying that i took good care of my words
they huddled at the core of a liana nest
fiery nucleus of a vegetal hedgehog
this is because for a long time i have taught them
to play with fire amidst fires
and to carry the last drop of saved water
to any one of the remote branchings of the sun
sun slumber
when i hear the first caravans of the sap going by
striving toward spring
oh to still be available

toward a delay of extinguished islands and volcanoes dozing

toron.
   taureau
      du fauve
         du rétiaire
            et l'heure et le péril
moi l'encordé du toujours
toujours dans la gorge
ce passé en boule non mâché
toujours ce lendemain noué
toujours notre rage aussi de ne savoir pas vivre
au fait faut-il savoir?
Féroces. c'est ça.
           nous définir féroces.
Avec le nous-mêmes.
Avec les hiers (pas bleus du tout)
avec demain inapaisé
         (des demains sans lendemains)
On enrage de n'avoir pas la vertu qui renonce
           Parlage.
                Parlure.
Le faire rétrécit
       laisse fumer le volcan.

let it smoke

torus.
   Taurus
     of the big game
       of the retiarius
         the hour and the peril
i the roped-in of forever
forever in my throat
this past in an unchewed mouthful
forever this knotted tomorrow
forever our rage as well not knowing how to live
but is it necessary to know?
Ferocious. that's it.
       to define ourselves as ferocious.
With the ourselves.
With the yesterdays (hardly blue at all)
with tomorrow unappeased
      (tomorrows without tomorrows)
It is maddening not to have the courage to give up
     Parley.
        Parlance.
Doing shrinks
   let the volcano smoke.

il y a des volcans qui se meurent
il y a des volcans qui demeurent
il y a des volcans qui ne sont là que pour le vent
il y a des volcans fous
il y a des volcans ivres à la dérive
il y a des volcans qui vivent en meutes et patrouillent
il y a des volcans dont la gueule émerge de temps en temps
véritables chiens de la mer
il y a des volcans qui se voilent la face
toujours dans les nuages
il y a des volcans vautrés comme des rhinocéros fatigués
dont on peut palper la poche galactique
il y a des volcans pieux qui élèvent des monuments
à la gloire des peuples disparus
il y a des volcans vigilants
des volcans qui aboient
montant la garde au seuil du Kraal des peuples endormis
il y a des volcans fantasques qui apparaissent et
    disparaissent
(ce sont jeux lémuriens)
il ne faut pas oublier ceux qui ne sont pas les moindres
les volcans qu'aucune dorsale n'a jamais repérés
et dont de nuit les rancunes se construisent
il y a des volcans dont l'embouchure est à la mesure
exacte de l'antique déchirure.

51

there are volcanoes that are dying
there are volcanoes that are extant
there are volcanoes that are only at home for the wind
there are crazed volcanoes
there are drunken adrift volcanoes
there are volcanoes that live in packs and patrol
there are volcanoes whose snouts emerge from time to time
veritable seadogs
there are volcanoes that veil their faces
always in the clouds
there are volcanoes as supine as weary rhinoceroses
whose galactic pouches can be probed
there are pious volcanoes that raise monuments
to the glory of extinct peoples
there are vigilant volcanoes
volcanoes that bark
mounting guard at the threshold of the Kraal of slumbering
   peoples
there are whimsical volcanoes that appear and disappear
(such are lemurian games)
and let us not forget last but not least
the volcanoes that no crest line has ever pinpointed
whose rancors build at night
there are volcanoes whose openings are in exact
scale with the ancient rip.

la loi des coraux

nous les chiffonniers de l'espoir
les porteurs du fameux chromosome
qui fait les écouteurs de géodes et d'hélodermes
nous de la dernière glane et des ondes de choc

s'il a attendu
le cœur battant et chaque fois plus absurde
chaque goutte de sang
s'il a bramé à la lisière d'être là
s'il s'est accroché furieusement
à un bouillonnement d'oiseaux loquaces
se disputant une carne dont
sa jeunesse est le trophée
s'il a senti à travers le vêtement émincé de la peau
chaque fois plus profonde la morsure du dieu
        (âge et son péage)
s'il a reconnu rôder autour de l'atoll qui s'épuise
le mollusque rongeur—la loi de ces coraux

du naufrage qu'une île s'explicite
selon une science d'oiseau-guide aguerri
        divaguant très tenace
vers les rochers sauvages de l'avenir.

law of the coral reefs

we the rag men of hope
carriers of the famous chromosome
that produces those who tune in to geodes and heloderms
we of the last gleaning and the shock waves

if he waited
his heart pounding and each beat more absurd
for each drop of blood
if he troated on the border of being there
if he hung on furiously
to a boiling of loquacious birds
fighting over some old bastard whose
trophy is his youth
if he felt through the threadbare garb of his skin
the god bite each time deeper
        (the toll of being old)
if he acknowledged the prowling of the gnawing mollusc
around the exhausted atoll—the law of these reefs

regarding the shipwreck let one island break away
according to the science of a toughened lead-bird
        wandering with great tenacity
toward the barbarous rocks of the future.

la force de regarder demain

les baisers des météorites
le féroce dépoitraillement des volcans à partir
de jeux d'aigle

la poussée des sous-continents arc-boutés
eux aussi aux passions sous-marines

la montagne qui descend ses cavalcades à grand galop
de roches contagieuses

ma parole capturant des colères
soleils à calculer mon être
        natif natal
                cyclopes violets des cyclones
n'importe l'insolent tison
        silex haut à brûler la nuit
épuisée d'un doute à renaître
la force de regarder demain

53

the strength to face tomorrow

the kisses of meteorites
the ferocious chest-bearing of volcanoes starting
with eagles' games

the push of subcontinents
also bracing themselves against underwater passions

the mountain that brings down its cavalcades in a full gallop
of contagious rocks

my words capturing angers
suns by which to reckon my native
     natal being
          violet cyclops of the cyclones
regardless of the arrogant brand
     flint high enough to torch the night
exhausted by a resurgent doubt
the strength to face tomorrow

quand
Miguel Angel Asturias
disparut

when
Miguel Angel Asturias
disappeared

quand Miguel Angel Asturias
disparut

bon batteur de silex
jeteur à toute volée de grains d'or dans l'épaisse
crinière de la nuit hippocampe
ensemenceur dément de diamants
brise-hache comme nul arbre dans la forêt
Miguel Angel s'asseyait à même le sol
disposant un grigri dans l'osselet de ses mots
quatre mots de soleil blanc
quatre mots de ceiba rouge
quatre mots de serpent corail

Miguel Angel se versait une rasade
de tafia d'étoiles macérées neuf nuits
à bouillir dans le gueuloir non éteint des volcans
et leur trachée d'obsidienne

Miguel Angel contemplait dans le fond de ses yeux
les graines montant gravement à leur profil d'arbres

Miguel Angel de sa plume caressait
la grande calotte des vents et le vortex polaire

Miguel Angel allumait de pins verts
les perroquets à tête bleue de la nuit

Miguel Angel perfusait d'un sang d'étoiles de lait
de veines diaprées et de ramages de lumières la grise
    empreinte
de l'heure du jour des jours du temps des temps

---

when Miguel Angel Asturias
disappeared

skillful flint striker
grandly flinging golden grain into the thick mane
of the hippocampal night
crazy diamond sower
       ax-breaker like no tree in the forest
Miguel Angel used to sit on the ground itself
arranging a grigri in the knucklebone of his words
       four words of white sun
       four words of red ceiba
       four words of coral snake

Miguel Angel poured a glassful
of astral tafia macerated nine nights
simmering in the nonexistent mugpiece of volcanoes
and their obsidian trachea

in the depths of his eyes Miguel Angel contemplated
seeds rising solemnly toward their arboreal contours

with his pen Miguel Angel caressed
the great skullcap of winds and the polar vortex

with green pines Miguel Angel ignited
the blue-headed parrots of the night

with a blood of milky stars of mottled veins and
floral designs of light Miguel Angel perfused the grey imprint
of the hour of the day of days of time of times

et puis
Miguel Angel déchaînait ses musiques sévères
une musique d'arc
une musique de vagues et de calebasses
une musique de gémissements de rivières
ponctuée des coups de canon des fruits du couroupite
et les burins de quartz se mettaient à frapper
les aiguilles de jade réveillaient les couteaux de silex
et les arbres à résine

ô Miguel Angel sorcier des vers luisants

le saman basculait empêtré de ses bras fous
avec toutes ses pendeloques de machines éperdues
avec le petit rire de la mer très doux
dans le cou chatouilleux des criques
et l'amitié minutieuse du Grand Vent

quand les flèches de la mort atteignirent Miguel Angel
on ne le vit point couché
mais bien plutôt déplier sa grande taille
au fond du lac qui s'illumina

Miguel Angel immergea sa peau d'homme
        et revêtit sa peau de dauphin

Miguel Angel dévêtit sa peau de dauphin
        et se changea en arc-en-ciel

Miguel Angel rejetant sa peau d'eau bleue
        revêtit sa peau de volcan

et s'installa montagne toujours verte
        à l'horizon de tous les hommes

                        and then
Miguel Angel unleashed his severe musics
a bowlike music
a music of waves and calabashes
a moaning river music
punctuated by the gunshots of sapucaia fruit
and the quartz chisels began to strike
the jade needles awakened the flint knives
and the resinous trees

O Miguel Angel you glowworm sorcerer

the shaman rocked entangled in his crazed arms
with all his pendants of frantic machines
with the very sweet chuckles of the sea
in the ticklish necks of coves
and the meticulous friendship of the High Wind

when the arrows of death reached Miguel Angel
he was not seen lying down
but rather unfolding his great height
at the bottom of the lake that burst into light

Miguel Angel immersed his human skin
            and donned his dolphin skin

Miguel Angel took off his dolphin skin
            and turned into a rainbow

Miguel Angel discarding his blue water skin
            donned his volcano skin

and settled, an ever green mountain,
            on the horizon of all men

Wifredo Lam

Wifredo Lam

Mantonica Wilson, ma marraine, avait le pouvoir de conjurer les éléments . . . Je l'ai visitée dans sa maison remplie d'idoles africaines. Elle m'a donnée la protection de tous ces dieux: de Yemanja, déesse de la mer, de Shango, dieu de la guerre compagnon d'Ogun-Ferraille, dieu du métal qui dorait chaque matin le soleil, toujours à côté d'Olorun, le dieu absolu de la création.

Wifredo Lam

Mantonica Wilson, my godmother, had the power to conjure the elements . . . I visited her in her house filled with African idols. She made me the gift of the protection of all these gods: of Yemanja, goddess of the sea, of Shango, god of war and companion of Ogun-Ferraille, god of metal who gilded the sun every morning, always at the side of Olorun, the absolute god of creation.

Wifredo Lam

rien de moins à signaler
que le royaume est investi
le ciel précaire
la relève imminente et légitime

rien sinon que le cycle des genèses vient sans préavis
d'exploser et la vie qui se donne sans filiation
le barbare mot de passe

rien sinon le frai frissonnant des formes qui se libèrent
des liaisons faciles
et hors de combinaisons trop hâtives s'évadent

mains implorantes
mains d'orantes
le visage de l'horrible ne peut être mieux indiqué
que par ces mains offusquantes

liseur d'entrailles et de destin violets
récitant de macumbas
mon frère
que cherches-tu à travers ces forêts
de cornes de sabots d'ailes de chevaux

toutes choses aiguës
toutes choses bisaiguës

to report: nothing less than
the kingdom under seige
the sky precarious
relief imminent and legitimate

nothing except that the cycle of geneses has just without
    warning
exploded as well as the life that gives itself
without filiation the barbarous password

nothing except the shivering spawn of forms liberating
    themselves
from facile bindings
and escaping from too premature combinings

imploring hands
hands in orison
the face of the horrible cannot be better indicated
than by these shocking hands

diviner of violet entrails and destiny
reciter of macumbas
my brother
what are you looking for throughout these forests
of horns of hooves of wings of horses

all punctuate things
all bipunctuate things

mais avatars d'un dieu animé au saccage
envol de monstres
j'ai reconnu aux combats de justice
le rare rire de tes armes enchantées
le vertige de ton sang
                    et la loi de ton nom.

avatars however of a god keen on destruction
monsters taking flight
in the combats of justice i recognized
the rare laughter of your magical weapons
the vertigo of your blood
                    and the law of your name.

toi diseur
    qu'y a-t-il à dire
    qu'y a-t-il à dire
y pourvoit la tête de l'hippotrague
y pourvoit le chasse-mouche

toi diseur
    qu'y a-t-il à dire
    qu'y a-t-il à dire
la vie à transmettre
la force à répartir
    et ce fleuve de chenilles

oh capteur
    qu'y a-t-il à dire
    qu'y a-t-il à dire
que le piège fonctionne
que la parole traverse

eh détrousseur
    eh ruseur
ouvreur de routes
laisse jalonner les demeures au haut réseau de la Mort
le sylphe bouffon de cette sylve

conversation
with Mantonica Wilson

you sayer
    what is there to say
    what is there to say
not already supplied by the hippotrague's head
not already supplied by the fly whisk

you sayer
    what is there to say
    what is there to say
life to transmit
strength to distribute
    and this stream of caterpillars

oh captor
    what is there to say
    what is there to say
that the snare works
that the word cuts through

hey highwayman
    hey trickster
opener of roads
let the grotesque sylph of this selva
stake out settlements in the upper network of Death

eh connaisseur du connaître
    par le couteau du savoir et le bec de l'oiseau
eh dégaineur
    par le couteau du sexe et l'oiseau calao
eh disperseur de voiles
    ici la croupe des femmes et le pis de la chèvre
ici
  ici
    ici
par tout œil écorcheur de crépuscules
l'orteil qui insiste
comme aux pistes de la nuit
    l'ardent sabot du cheval-vent

to know, he says

hey connoisseur of knowing
    through the knife of knowledge and the beak of the bird
hey unsheather
    through the knife of the penis and the calao
hey disperser of veils
    here is the woman's rump and the goat's udder
here
    here
        here
through any eye flayer of sunsets
the toe that probes on
as do the ardent hooves of the wind-horse
    along the trails of night

genèse pour Wifredo

plus d'aubier
rien qu'une aube d'os purs
des os qui explosent grand champ
des os qui explosent aux quatre vents
des os qui dansent à peine jaillis du sillon
des os qui crient qui hurlent
qu'on n'en perde
        qu'on n'en perde aucun
des os qui par rage se sont emparés
de tout ce qu'il reste de vie

de sang il ne sinue que juste
celui médian d'un verbe parturiant

genesis for Wifredo

no more alburnum
only a dawn of pure bones
bones that explode open field
bones that explode to the four quarters
bones that dance barely out of the furrow
bones that shriek that howl
let's not lose
        not lose any of them
bones that enraged have seized
all that is left of life

as for blood there's only a sinuous thread
in the median of a parturient verb

clé de voûte
  hiéroglyphes
peu importe la constellation abolie
jamais resserrée l'infinie combinatoire
avertir déborde
le noyau parle
  impossible l'erreur
  difficile l'errance
le hochet directionnel pend aux arbres
à portée de toute main
le losange veille les yeux fermés
ici commence
  repris aux fauves
le territoire sacré mal concédé des feuilles

keystone
      hieroglyphs
forget the abolished constellation
never recompressed the infinite combinative
overflows warning
the nucleus is speaking
      no error possible
      errancy difficult
the directional rattle hangs from the tree   *
within reach of anyone
the lozenge keeps watch with closed eyes   *
here begins
      reclaimed from wild beasts
the sacred territory reluctantly conceded by the leaves

        (la nécessité de la spéciation
        n'étant acceptée que dans la mesure
        où elle légitime les plus audacieuses transgressions)
passer dit-il
        et que dure chaque meurtrissure
passer
        mais ne pas dépasser les mémoires vivantes
passer
        (penser est trop rapide)
de tout paysage garder intense la transe
        du passage
passer
        anabase et diabase
déjà
se dégage du fouillis au loin
tribulation d'un volcan
la halte d'une vive termitière

  (the necessity of speciation
  acceptable only in that
  it legitimizes the most audacious transgressions)
pass on he says
  and let each bruise last
pass on
  but do not trespass on living memories
pass on
  (thinking happens too quickly)
keep the trance of passage of every landscape
  intense
pass on
  anabasis and diabasis
in the distance
a volcano's tribulation
the halt of a lively termitarium
is already emerging from the muddle

en ce temps-là le temps était l'ombrelle d'une femme très
    belle
au corps de maïs aux cheveux de déluge
en ce temps-là la terre était insermentée
en ce temps-là le cœur du soleil n'explosait pas
(on était très loin de la prétintaille quinteuse
qu'on lui connaît depuis)
en ce temps-là les rivières se parfumaient incandescentes
en ce temps-là l'amitié était un gage
pierre d'un soleil qu'on saisissait au bond
en ce temps-là la chimère n'était pas clandestine
ce n'était pas davantage une échelle de soie contre un mur
contre le Mur
alors vint un homme qui jetait comme cauris ses couleurs
et faisait revivre vive la flamme des palimpsestes
alors vint un homme dont la défense lisse
était un masque goli
et le verbe un poignard acéré
alors un homme vint qui se levait contre la nuit du temps
un homme stylet
un homme scalpel
un homme qui opérait des taies
c'était un homme qui s'était longtemps tenu
entre l'hyène et le vautour
au pied d'un baobab
un homme vint
un homme vent
un homme vantail

in those days time was the sunshade of a very beautiful
  woman
with a maize body and a deluge of hair
in those days the earth was nonjuring
in those days the sun's heart did not explode
(we were a long way from the crotchety frills
we've known ever since)
in those days rivers used an incandescent perfume
in those days friendship was a pledge
stone from a sun caught on the bounce
in those days the chimera was not clandestine
nor was it a silk ladder against a wall
against the Wall
then came a man who threw his colors around like cowrie
  shells
and who revived the vivid flame of palimpsests
then came a man whose polished cover
was a goli mask   *
and whose verb was a sharpened dagger
then came a man who stood up against the night of time
a stiletto man
a scalpel man
a man who operated on leucomas
he was a man who had for a long time held himself
between hyena and vulture
at the base of a baobab
a man came
a hurricane man   *

un homme portail
le temps n'était pas un gringo gringalet
je veux dire un homme rabordaille
                    un homme vint
un homme

a ligative man
an adventive man
time was not a gangly gringo
i mean a second adventivity man
                    a man came
a man

que l'on présente son cœur
au soleil

la Bête a dû céder sur le sentier de ton dernier défi

Bête aux abois
Mort traquée par la mort
de son masque déchu elle s'arc-boute à son mufle

solaire
l'œuf la suit à la piste

l'aile du tout-à-coup jaillit

la victoire est d'offrir à la gourde des germes
le sexe frais du temps
sur l'aube d'une main mendiante de fantômes

let us offer its heart to
the sun

the Beast must have surrendered on the path of your last
    challenge

Beast at bay
Death cornered by death
with its fallen mask it leans against its muzzle

solar
the egg is following its tracks

the wing of all-at-once flashes

victory consists in offering the fresh penis of time
to the gourd of seeds
in the dawn of a hand begging for ghosts

tant pis si la forêt se fane en épis de pereskia
tant pis si l'avancée est celle des fourmis tambocha
tant pis si le drapeau ne se hisse qu'à des hampes desséchées
tant pis
       tant pis
si l'eau s'épaissit en latex vénéneux
préserve la parole
rends fragile l'apparence
capte aux décors le secret des racines
la résistance ressuscite
autour de quelques fantômes plus vrais que leur allure
                       insolites bâtisseurs

incongruous builders

too bad if the forest wilts into Pereskia stalks
too bad if the advance is that of tambocha ants   *
too bad if the flag is hoisted only on a withered pole
too bad
      too bad
if the water thickens into poisonous latex
protect the word
render appearance fragile
capture in scenery the secret of roots
the resistance resurrects
around a few ghosts more real than they appear
                    incongruous builders

il n'est pas question de livrer le monde aux assassins d'aube
      la vie-mort
      la mort-vie
les souffleteurs de crépuscule
les routes pendent à leur cou d'écorcheurs
comme des chaussures trop neuves
il ne peut s'agir de déroute
seuls les panneaux ont été de nuit escamotés
pour le reste
des chevaux qui n'ont laissé sur le sol
que leurs empreintes furieuses
des mufles braqués de sang lapé
le dégainement des couteaux de justice
et des cornes inspirées
des oiseaux vampires tout bec allumé
se jouant des apparences
mais aussi des seins qui allaitent des rivières
et les calebasses douces au creux des mains d'offrande

une nouvelle bonté ne cesse de croître à l'horizon

new kindness

to deliver the world to the assassins of dawn is out of the
   question
         death-life
         life-death
those who slap dusk in the face
roads hang from their flayer necks
like shoes too new
we're not dealing with a rout
only the traps have been whisked away during the night
as for the rest
horses that have left nothing more in the ground
than their furious hoofprints
muzzles aimed with lapped-up blood
the unsheathing of the knives of justice
and of the inspired horns
of vampire birds their entire beaks lit up
defying appearances
but also breasts nursing rivers
and sweet calabashes in the hollows of offering hands

a new kindness is ceaselessly growing on the horizon

Translators' Notes

P. 85: *porana:* a climbing herb of East Africa, Madagascar, Asia, and Australia, of the convolvulaceae family.

P. 105: *touaou:* neither we nor our consultants have been able to identify this term.

P. 105: *couresse:* popular term for the nonvenomous Martinican water snake. When swimming, the couresse holds its head out of the water. "Proud as a couresse crossing a river" is a popular saying.

P. 107: *Maré Maré:* a game adult slaves played, involving tying up the players. The last to be tied was the winner.

P. 117: *anguillard:* common name for Proteus, probably based on *anguille* (eel).

P. 123: *Compitalia:* in Roman religion, the *lares compitales* were the guardians of the crossroads and the junctions of fields, in whose honor were held the celebration of the *Laralia* or *Compitalia.*

P. 131: *parakimomène:* possibly a misremembered Greek word, *parakinouménos,* a present middle/passive participle, meaning very disturbed or very agitated. Our word is based on parakinesia, which refers to a motor irregularity due to a nervous disorder.

P. 135: *Shango:* see Césaire's contextualization of this word in the passage quoted from Wifredo Lam at the beginning of the last section of this book; Shango is an important orisha in Brazilian macumba and in Afro-Caribbean religions.

P. 147: *malfini:* see earlier note on *menfenil,* p. 73.

P. 153: *recado:* the French *récade* appears to be a form of the Spanish *recado,* meaning a complimentary message or a gift.

P. 167: *poui:* a Trinidadian Creole word for the tree Tabebuia Pallida, with pink trumpet-shaped flowers.

P. 175: *through-my-fault crab:* "a crab having one very small and one very large claw, which latter it carries folded up against its body, so as to have suggested the idea of a penitent striking his bosom, and uttering the sacramental words of the Catholic confession, 'Through my fault, through my fault, through my most grievous fault.'" (Lafcadio Hearn, *Two Years in the French West Indies* [New York: Harpers, 1890], p. 141).

P. 185: *zopilote:* in Mexican Spanish, a buzzard.

P. 193: *unbroken nigger crest line:* our phrase, based on the French title *dorsale bossale.* We understand *bossale* to be an adjective based on a word (*bozal* in Spanish) that refers to a slave just arrived straight from Africa, and who has not been baptized and tamed. It carries a sense of wild or savage, as in *le parler bossale* (crude speech).

P. 219: *directional rattle:* according to Maryse Condé in a personal communication to the translators, "le hochet directionnel" refers to the voudou Vèvè cult, and is a hollow rattle used by a priest to beat a rhythm. The Creole word for it is *asson.* Condé tells us that the *lozenge* (in the same poem, two lines later) is a diamond-shaped figure drawn with white chalk on the floor of a voudou temple.

P. 223: *second adventivity:* our phrase is based on Césaire's coined word *rabordaille.* He seems to have added the pre-

i, laminaria . . .

fix *re-* (again) as well as the suffix *-aille* (which exists in many words referring to communal rituals such as *fiançailles, ripailles,* etc.) to the verb *aborder* (to land or approach land). On the basis of the special kind of man who appears in this poem, a kind of culture-bringer or savior, we constructed our phrase.

P. 223: *goli:* according to the *Dictionnaire Bambara-Français* by H. Bazin (Paris, 1906; reprinted Ridgewood: N.J.: Gress Press, 1965), *goli* is Bambara patois for *boli* (a grigri, or fetish).

P. 223: *a man came:* the next three lines, as well as the fifth line, have not been translated literally, as Césaire's French indicates that the choice of key words in these lines is based on sound plays leading to *rabordaille.* These three lines follow "un homme vint" (a man came). Here is the French (with the key sounds underlined) next to a literal English version:

un homme *vent*	a wind man
un homme *vantail*	a folding-door man
un homme *portail*	a portal man
. . .	. . .
. . . un homme ra*bordaille*	. . . a re-approach land-ity man

P. 229: *tambocha:* according to Condé, ants also known as toc-toc ants, whose bite is painful.